The Journey Within

IMRE VALLYON

Sounding-Light

The Journey Within by Imre Vallyon
First edition, May 2015

ISBN 978-0-909038-70-0

Sounding-Light Publishing Ltd.
PO Box 771, Hamilton 3240, New Zealand
www.soundinglight.com

Chapter 1 is excerpted from the author's book *Planetary Transformation* (2010).
Chapters 10, 11 and 12 are excerpted from *The Magical Mind* (1989).

CONTENTS

~

A NOTE ON SANSKRIT USAGE
~

The Sanskrit language is SAṄSKṚTA, meaning "well-made, perfectly polished". It is also called DEVANĀGARĪ, "God's writing". It is the most ancient sacerdotal (priestly) language of India, used for writing the scriptures, mythologies and sciences of the ancient Indian Subcontinent.

Sanskrit is a multi-layered language. It is a language which has the highest number of esoteric, spiritual and religious words, terms and expressions. There is no other language like it on Earth. The spiritual and esoteric terms run into thousands and thousands.

This work describes the pronunciation of the Sanskrit words by way of transliterated spellings, along with esoteric and spiritual meanings, as perceived in Higher Consciousness. Note that usage will in general vary from popular adaptations. The Sanskrit word KARMA, for instance, translates literally as "action" and may refer either to a cosmic principle (action and reaction, cause and effect) or to one's accumulated *karmas* or "actions".

To help preserve their original sound-structures, Sanskrit words are pluralized using a small 's' (Nirmāṇakāyas), except for those commonly used in English (mantras, gurus). A pronunciation guide can be found at the back of the book.

EDITOR'S NOTE

~

The *Journey Within* is a print-only compilation of ebooks from the Spiritual Path series by Imre Vallyon. It offers the reader a selection of universal spiritual knowledge and understanding to inspire and light the way for those wishing to follow a spiritual path in today's world. As each ebook in the series is a self-contained publication on a particular aspect of the Spiritual Path, the reader may notice some repetition from chapter to chapter, especially in regard to the explanation of the inner nature of the human being and the Cosmos.

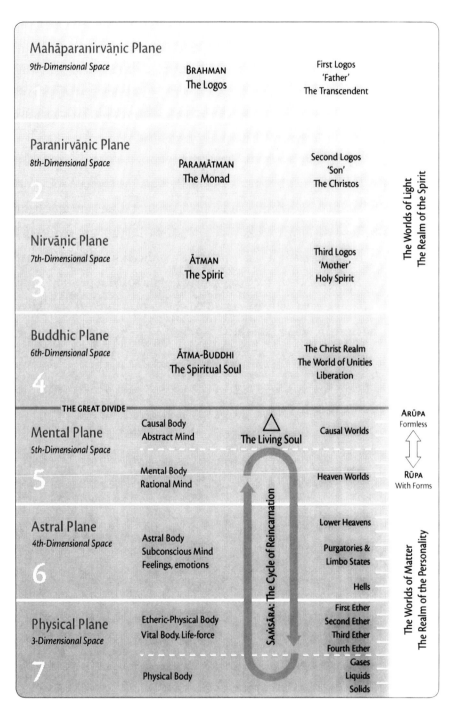

The Seven Great Planes of Being

Introduction

The Importance of Right Knowledge

People act according to their knowledge; whatever knowledge they have is the starting point of their action. There are tribes in the Amazon that still hunt with bows and arrows. Their vocabulary is limited to several hundred words and because their knowledge is limited their action field is limited. Basically, you cannot do any more than what you know and this is true whether you live in the First World, the Third World or in a primitive tribe. Your knowledge is you and that is your limitation: little knowledge, little action; big knowledge, big action; vast knowledge, vast action.

If you live in a so-called developed country and go to school and only get a basic education, you are often limited to doing low-paying jobs. With more education, however, you expand your knowledge field, so you can get a better job. As far as the world is concerned, therefore, education is a wonderful thing because it expands your possibilities and helps you have a better life. So even on the worldly level, knowledge is important; the more you know, the more possibilities you have.

If you are a religious person you have been brought up in a certain knowledge-field, given to you by your religion, so you act according to that knowledge. If you are a good Roman Catholic you act according to how a good Roman Catholic lives; if you are a good Muslim you act according to how a good Muslim lives. So even the ordinary knowledge-field of any religion—provided of course that the religion has reasonably sane ideas, not the insane ideas of a fundamentalist religion—gives you a much broader understanding of life than the purely materialistic view. This is because even the most basic religious ideas include the existence of a soul and of God, that there is life after death, and these extend your possibility of action. In other words, religious people at least know that when they die they go to a heaven world or some place or another, that they survive beyond death. That in itself will help them, because when they leave their physical body they will know that they are going somewhere.

In the next stage of knowledge, you come to a point when, although you may be religious, you begin to question religion, to question how much of what the priests, swamis and monks say is true: does God really exist, does the Soul really exist, does Heaven exist, does Hell exist? This is good because you are now entering the seeking stage, which is where you have to understand the importance of *Right Knowledge*.

This is because many people at this stage get sidetracked and try to develop psychic powers, like clairvoyance, the ability to see psychic phenomena, or clairaudience, the ability to hear the spirits on the Astral World. They think that they know more than the religious people and more than the materialistic people. It is true that their knowledge is slightly better because they can see or hear one of the invisible worlds (in this case, the Astral World), but it is still only about the lower regions of the inner dimensions. It is a higher form of knowledge, yes, but it's not the Right Knowledge.

Then there are the Buddhist philosophers, the Vedantic and other Hindu philosophers, and even some Western philosophers who say that you are the Self, Ātman, the Spirit, that there is an absolute state from which we all came and to which we will all return. This is a high form of knowledge but it is still only an intellectual knowledge. It will help those philosophers when they die and move into the next world, because they have high-frequency minds and will be attracted to the Higher Mind Worlds, the true Heaven Worlds, where they will enjoy

Soul revelations on the nature of Divinity and so on. But although it is much higher than all the previous levels of knowledge, it is still not the Right Knowledge.

So what is the Right Knowledge?

The basis of the Right Knowledge is that knowledge is unlimited, experience is unlimited. Some people awaken Kuṇḍalinī; they experience something and that's it. Some people practise Haṭha Yoga or Rāja Yoga techniques and experience something and that's it. Sectarian groups like the Hare Krishnas or the Mormons work along a particular knowledge line, an understanding they have about themselves and about God, and they use one particular mantra or system of thought. But they become defined by the energy of that mantra or system of thought, and they cannot move beyond it. They are stuck and cannot evolve because to be able to evolve, your mind and heart must be open, not based on one idea or one stream of thought, one kind of practice, one kind of energy.

In other words, what you know you practise, but what you practise you experience, and that becomes your limitation. No knowledge is final; no experience is final. If one particular experience were the final experience possible, the evolution of human consciousness would stop. It would get locked up in that experience for the rest of eternity—a Buddhist would experience the Void, a Christian would experience God sitting on a throne with Jesus next to him and the Holy Spirit hovering like a dove.

If you meditate regularly and live a spiritual life, you may feel bliss or an all-consuming love or see an infinite void or see all the inner worlds, and you may think that your experience is the final goal, that you are now a Buddha or a Christ, that you have reached the end of human evolution—but it was just an experience; one day you will go further. So real knowledge is infinite. Real experience is infinite. Nothing that people experience is the Infinite; it only *points* towards the Infinite.

When you have the Right Knowledge, therefore, no matter what technique, process, meditation or practice you use, you do not get stuck in that process, technique or mode of understanding; you always remain open for the Spirit to act inside you, spontaneously. The Right Knowledge is the knowledge that leads to true Liberation, which is a state of infinite consciousness that transcends individual experiences and stays with you forever, whether you are in the body or out of the body, whether you are in this world, the next world or in any realm of existence. The Right Knowledge is therefore the *Saving Knowledge*, the knowledge that leads to Eternal Consciousness—an infinite possibility of *knowing*, an infinite possibility of *experiencing*, an infinite possibility of *becoming*.

In a word, the Right Knowledge, the Saving Knowledge, is precisely what you need for the Journey Within. ✶

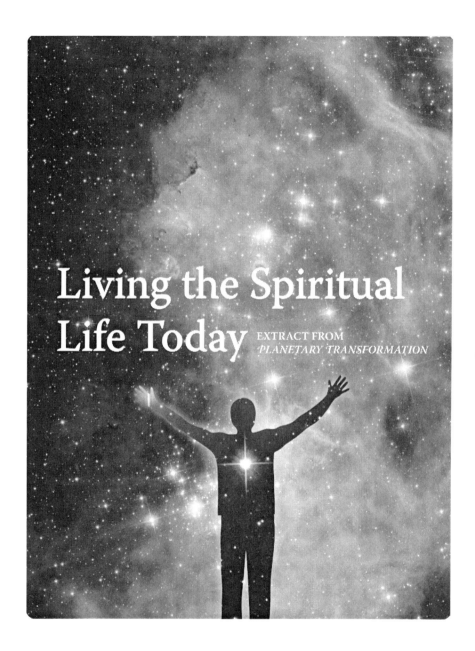

Living the Spiritual Life Today

EXTRACT FROM
PLANETARY TRANSFORMATION

CHAPTER 1

"*Within* *us is another dimension, another vast, bright,*
imperishable Reality, full of Ecstasy, Joy, Potential and Creativity
beyond imagination, and we don't even want to know about it!"

The Search for Reality

The human being is a complicated creature. We consist of two major parts: the totally spiritual and the totally material. By the *material* part, I mean the physical body (the temporary manifestation into which you have incarnated in this particular lifetime), your emotional nature, your thinking nature and the life-energy inside you. The other part of you, the *spiritual* part, does not incarnate and is always the same. You may call it the Soul, the Spirit, or the Divinity within you.

In this extremely materialistic society in which we are living, there is too much emphasis on physical things, on physical comforts and enjoyment, on mental creativity and thinking for its own sake. With all that busyness of society, the *spiritual* part of us—that which has existed since the beginning of time and which will exist until the end of time and beyond—is completely forgotten. Of all the people in the world, how many are desperately seeking the spiritual part of themselves? Thousands maybe, but what is that compared to the seven billion on this planet?

To use an analogy: imagine you have fifteen million euros in a Swiss bank account. Your parents gave it to you but somehow you know nothing about it, and meanwhile you continue to live as a homeless person, sleeping at the railway station and thinking you are miserable and unhappy. Similarly, we each have this incredible Spiritual Reality within us—we are omniscient, omnipresent, omnipotent, full of absolute Bliss, Love, Joy, Ecstasy and vibrant living—and we know nothing about it! Furthermore, we are not even interested in seeking it, because we are so entrapped in material pursuits or personality satisfaction— the satisfaction of the physical body, the mind and the emotions.

Within us is another dimension, another vast, bright, imperishable Reality, full of Ecstasy, Joy, Potential and Creativity beyond imagination, and we don't even want to know about it! This is the disaster of modern society. And because we have forgotten the essential Self, the *real Being* within ourselves, we have wars and stress in society; we have family problems, work problems, political and religious problems. We are not connected to our Spiritual Source; we are completely out of tune with Reality and will continue to have problems until the end of time unless we realize that our society is completely off the rails. We are looking for solutions at the level of the personality—psychological, sociological, philosophical and political explanations—but they never have solved the problem and never will. They cannot solve the problem because they only revolve around this limited expression of reality.

What we see in this world is only a fragment of Creation. The vast *physical* Universe is literally just the surface or skin of the multidimensional, infinite Space. People do not seem bothered to seek this multidimensional, almighty part of Nature and that great, almighty part of themselves.

However, those people who have started on the Spiritual Path have seen beyond that limited view of reality and believe there is something inside them that is greater, something well worth seeking. You may call it Self-Realization, the Realization of Truth, the Realization of God, the Realization of Nirvāṇa, of the Buddha-Mind or the Kingdom of Heaven. That belief is an indication that people are searching within for the greater part of themselves and the greater part of the Cosmos—that which they cannot see.

There are more than a billion Christians and more than a billion Muslims, and many millions of Jews, Buddhists and other religious people in the world, but I am not referring here to religious people. You can be religious through habit. You may have been brought up as a Roman Catholic, so you go to church, or if you were brought up as a Jew you go to the synagogue, but that doesn't mean you are seeking the Eternal at all. In Buddhist countries you see boys as young as four years of age put into monasteries and they live all their lives as monks, but they are only monks because they were put there. If they had been born in Western Europe and given a computer job, that is what they would be doing. Just because they put on a monk's robe through social habit or culture doesn't mean they are real monks, that they are truly seeking Reality. You have to distinguish between what is simply habit and something that is *desperate* inside you, desperate *to want to know and experience the truth in this lifetime.* Whether religious or not, until a person has reached that desperate stage, he or she cannot progress far.

If you are at the beginning stage, you might think that you meditate or chant because it relaxes you, or because it harmonizes your mind and makes you feel happy and alive. Well, that is fine; it does do those things. But if you still have such ideas—that meditation or chanting is only useful for dealing with the stresses of life—then you are still scratching the surface. You have not really understood the process. It is only when you desperately want that invisible *Otherness* inside you that the need to meditate or chant will make sense to you.

You need to live a spiritual life to attain the Spiritual Dimension. You have to structure your whole life in a spiritual way, according to a plan, otherwise you simply won't get there. If you want to go by train from Paris to Moscow, you have to take a specific route. You get on a specific train and then others until you finally arrive in Moscow. Similarly, you cannot attain Enlightenment haphazardly. To attain the Buddha-Nature, or God-Consciousness, you need to understand where you are going and exactly what you need to do to get there.

Something has to take place inside you. You may wake up one day and say, "I am going to find the Truth. I know it is there and I will find it in *this* lifetime, *now.*" It is possible to do that, but only for those who make a real effort, which means that you must have that desire, that inner attunement, twenty-four hours a day, not just during a chanting or meditation session.

When you learn music, ballet dancing, or any art or sport, you have to practise for hours every day. Not only that, your mind works on it all the time, day and night. Everywhere you travel, you often see business-men at airports and hotels constantly using their cell phones and lap-top computers. They succeed because they are focused on their work, twenty-four hours a day. The business people understand that only through effort will they gain worldly success. Nobody in this world will succeed with an occasional effort—it is impossible. It is exactly the same in spiritual life: either you totally throw yourself into it or you don't. But spiritual disciples think, "Well, I'll think about it; maybe when I retire. Just before I die I'll call upon God and God will save me." No, God won't save you. Either you dedicate yourself to it or you won't get there. That has been the ancient law since Creation began. So ask yourself: "Am I really serious about spiritual life? Am I really interested in it, or is it just something that is nice to do occasionally?"

The Original Spiritual Path

When you take up this Path it is important to understand that it is the *real* Spiritual Path, the one that has been suppressed for thousands of years. About six thousand years ago, just after the great Vedic civiliza-tion in India, the Spiritual Science was practised by kings, dictators, soldiers, emperors—people with tremendous worldly power who lived *in* society. They were powerful people, yet they practised the Spiritual Path totally. They did not divide their worldly duties and worldly power from their spiritual lives. Then around three thousand years ago came the silly idea that to become an enlightened being—a YOGĪ, a Mystic or a Saint—you had to leave the world behind, leave your family, your job, your duties, and shut yourself in an ashram or in a cave. You had to completely negate yourself (your mind, emotions, and body) and disconnect yourself from society.

That wrong teaching became the ideal spiritual way of life and it is still being practised in India today. It was also practised in the Prophetic Schools of the West, by the Christian Fathers in the desert. Everybody started practising this idea that to be spiritual you had to get rid of your personal mechanism and your connection with the world, to somehow just be in a vacuum, crazily desiring God and using all kinds of techniques to attain. Unfortunately, that idea pervaded the East as well as the West. It was completely wrong then and it is still wrong now.

To live a spiritual life, you don't have to give up your job or become a monk or a nun. The spiritual life is where you are, whether or not you have a job, are married or have children. You don't have to suddenly throw everything away and rush off to join a Tibetan monastery. In fact, you would most likely find that you couldn't be a Tibetan or Buddhist monk even if you wanted to, because you don't have the makeup for it. It is silly to try to become something other than what you are. If you live in Switzerland, the way for you is in Switzerland; in Vietnam, the way is in Vietnam. We always have this idea that by becoming something else we will become spiritual. *The Kingdom of Heaven is within you.* You do not have to travel anywhere to find it.

Everything that is spiritual is already within you; you can find the Kingdom of God inside yourself, right now. God is not just in a church, a mosque or a synagogue. The idea that God is at a particular place is false, because God is everywhere, so the trick with spiritual life is to realize that what you are seeking is where you are. If you are in the garden or in the kitchen, you can find God there. It is so simple *if* you understand that God is omnipotent, omniscient, omnipresent, and that your Soul is omnipotent, omniscient, omnipresent. If both God and your Soul are omnipresent, they must be in the same place—and they are. You cannot find what is within you if you are continually looking outwards.

So choose your path, wherever you are. It makes no difference whether you live in an apartment or a palace; God is wherever you are and that is where you must find God. It is simple if you can come to this realization: the Divine Presence is omnipresent and your Soul is omnipresent. The two are one.

You need to make this radical turnaround inside yourself and realize that your outer life is only self-maintenance to keep you going in this physical dimension. If your outer life is your only focus, you will keep going in this dimension until you die; then you will circulate for a little while in the inner dimensions (in the Limbo state, the Hell Worlds or the Heaven Worlds); then you will come back into incarnation and live a material life as you have done for thousands of lifetimes already. In the East they call this SAṀSĀRA, the Wheel of Life. But if you realize that this endless circulation is not the meaning of life, then what *is* the meaning of life?

If you look at a turning wheel you will see that it revolves around its hub, the central point. Inside us, that central point is based in the Heart Chakra, around which everything revolves. But there is a part of the Heart Chakra, much deeper within, that does not revolve. This is our central point that is always in the "is" condition, the eternal state of Being. If you can find that, you are enlightened, you are a Buddha or a Christ, and you can walk liberated and free amongst Humankind.

You can find it in the battle of life. Furthermore, every encounter you have in life is an aspect of God because everything is a manifestation of the Divine Nature—whether it be a candle, a flower, your son, your grandmother, or a vast star-system or galaxy. They are all simply particles of the great Ocean of Life.

You are part of that great Ocean of Life, the amazing Play of God (LĪLĀ, in Sanskrit), so why get bogged down in the little details of life? Somebody may have insulted you forty years ago and you are still annoyed with that person, still telling your children and grand-children about it. But since that occasion you have moved millions of kilometres through space; time has changed, energies have changed, the whole universe has changed, and you are still holding on to a silly incident of the past. While we hold on to the past—whether as an individual, a family, a nation or a religion—we are holding back the progress of the planet. Forget what happened in the past; always move ahead. The Truth is here now.

If you could concentrate one hundred percent in this very moment, you would attain Enlightenment. You would see the Ocean of Reality inside everything and everyone, penetrating every atom of space.

The average person thinks that Enlightenment is something only a few people have attained in Tibet or in a cave in the Himalayas. It is not so; you can attain it too. The only difference is that those few people believed they could attain it, and they did. The sooner people attune themselves to the great Plan behind everything, the sooner they get there. Some people like walking, some people like running, some take a bike or even a luxury car. But some people do better—they take an aeroplane. So it is in the spiritual life: either you plunge in, totally immerse yourself and awaken within, or you take the slow route and occasionally think about it.

I want to inspire you to search, but to search with honesty. Open your Heart a hundred percent to Reality, because it is already here. Don't delay, saying, "Oh, I'm too busy now, I will do it when I retire." You have to do it now. Delaying that seeking of the Truth until later does not work because the Truth is exactly where you are right now—in your office, in your home, anywhere. Don't say, "Now I'm not spiritual because I'm working in the office, but when I'm chanting I'm spiritual." *You are spiritual all the time!* The Spirit is literally everywhere: you can pick up a flower and it is there, you can look at the face of a person and it is there, you can look at the sky or the Sun and it is there. You can find God everywhere.

The next time you are arguing with your husband, wife, child or boss, just think of him or her as an image of God. If you could see the other person in that way, then suddenly the argument will fade out and that person will become something much larger because you are tuning into the person's Soul. Every Soul is an absolutely beautiful, bright entity, an Angel of Light, quite literally. On the Soul level you see the personality mechanism as only a covering, a veil. The Latin word persona means "a mask", and the personality is simply a mask. How you *appear* to other people is not you; it is just your mask. If they could see the real you, they would go into shock! They would see you as a beautiful, radiant Being of Light.

The mask of your personality enables you to deal with this world, in this particular space and time, and that is all. But the *real* you is like the Christ or the Buddha: a god incarnate on this planet. So you have to remember that this is what you really are and *live* it. You *can* do it because you *are* that already. Drop the mask of the personality every now and then and begin to live like a Divine Being, rather than identifying with what people say about you. Forget what people say about you—whether or not you are beautiful, whether you are good or bad. It is just their opinion of you. It is not you. Furthermore, any opinion you may have of them is not them either. It is simply one personality judging another personality, one mask judging another mask. That is all.

To be able to influence people in a positive, harmonious way, you first have to go through a transformation yourself. *You have to awaken inside first.* When you are awake, it is like awakening into another universe, another reality, another truth-condition. You are not *thinking* about anything. It is an awakening to every possibility of the moment, here, now. From then on, everything that happens to you is part of a grand miracle and you see a great design behind it. Even what appears to be unpleasant or limiting, you see as part of a grand design, and the culmination of that design is always goodness. You understand that no matter how silly human behaviour may be, the end result is always good and the final destiny of everything is pure joy, happiness and Light.

The Stage of Doubt

You may wake up one day and know that things are not right on this Physical Plane, and you begin to allow your inner consciousness to be influenced by the environment or the natural forces around you. You may be doing nicely—having periods of deep meditation with inner experiences and Inspiration—and then suddenly the worldly circumstances and problems of life become too much for you and you begin to doubt. Then you might say to yourself, "If God is real then these things should not be happening, and especially not to me! If the Teaching is true then I should be in a blissed-out, transcendental state and none of this negativity should touch me!"

Many people come to this stage of doubt on their spiritual journey. It is sometimes called the stage of *dryness* or the *desert condition.* The inner forces are not strong enough to neutralize the forces outside you, and usually the worldly forces outside you are very strong! It could be your family or it could be your job, your environment, your relationships, or society in general. It could be the result of wars, famine or natural disasters—there are hundreds of possibilities! You become immersed in it all. You become overwhelmed and give up hope.

This phase of doubt is not new. There were doubters amongst the followers of Jesus (Thomas, for example), the followers of Buddha and Krishna, the followers of all Teachers. That doubt is real; it is a psychological condition. It has nothing to do with the Teaching, the Teacher, the Path or anything else. It is simply a personality problem. The personality becomes overwhelmed by negative, imperfect or unhealthy conditions and at that moment one's Soul-connection weakens.

For instance, you may have a good meditation; the Light of the Soul comes down and "tickles" the personality and you feel everything is fine. You can put up with wars, earthquakes, floods, disasters or the Universe dissolving! But sometimes, because the seething mass of materialistic energy around you is contrary to the Soul-Nature, the Light of the Soul cannot penetrate the personality and you begin to doubt. People having this experience might give up and re-establish themselves in the world comfortably and think they have found the real purpose of life.

Associated with every Teacher, in every period of history, were people who failed to continue on the Spiritual Path. They were originally inspired by the Path, by the Teaching, by the Teacher, and were enthusiastic, but then the personal hassles became too much. Remember that those personal hassles are real. They are not only part of your Karma, but also of the mass World Karma. You have not caused all the problems of the world, but you are a small part of the bigger problems of the world which were created by everyone.

In previous times it was not such a problem if people became overwhelmed and left the Spiritual Path, but you cannot afford to "switch off" nowadays because you do not have much time. The planet is not becoming more blissed-out! In fact, it is likely there will be increasing counterproductive and opposing forces, so if you switch off now you will be off track for this particular lifetime and obviously will not come out of this whole trip well.

I am letting you know this because you *will* go through it, if you have not already—especially when you find life to be tough and you feel that you don't have the psychic strength or energy to deal with spiritual life anymore. That is a dangerous time because if you follow that track you literally lose your Soul-connection, and to re-establish it becomes very difficult, especially if bigger problems come along.

It is important that you practise feeling the sense of Spiritual Reality in your daily life. For instance, if you are able to feel oneness through Nature, wherever you seek Nature you will feel oneness there. If you are able to feel oneness with people during a meditation or chanting session, when you go into the world you will be able to feel oneness with people at work or wherever you go. You must practise that continuum of consciousness, so you don't feel that the world is "out there" and you are here, with no connection with the world.

Finding Balance in Spiritual Life

If you are one of those people who are always busy and have no energy left at the end of the day to meditate or to think of spiritual things, then try reducing your workload. You have to change something in your life, and that is not selfish. Many people have this idea that it is selfish or "not spiritual" to look after yourself, but it is simply common sense. If you cannot help yourself, then in time you will crack up and you won't be able to help others. To benefit others you have to be in a reasonably good condition yourself.

As a student of Wisdom you have to reassess what you do twenty-four hours a day—how much you run around after others, where you are spending your energy, what workload you can reduce—so that you can still do your meditation and remain attuned to the Light of the Soul. This is very important. With the way society is heading, there will be increasingly greater demands placed upon you, so you need to be wise and accept that you cannot save, heal or fix everybody.

Every personality is a limited construct; it is not an infinite powerhouse. So accept your limitation without feeling guilty, work with it and adjust it to make sure that the Light functions inside you at all times. Then, if your life is equalized and balanced, with fewer ups and downs, you will find that the Light of the Soul can flow steadily and you will feel that steady Inspiration from within at all times, no matter where you are or what you are doing. Then everything you do in life will have a momentous effect on other people. You won't have to give them big sermons; because of your inner Being, your very presence will change them. Wherever you go, you will touch the lives of many and you will find that your ability to serve others will increase. It is important to understand this principle, because the coming years will be difficult and many people may want to give up the Spiritual Path because they think life is too much to handle.

The rule is that you don't have to save the whole world all by yourself. Because there are millions of starving people in Africa, don't think that you have to feed them all, or that you have to heal the many sick people in India all by yourself. It is a naive, "do-gooder" idea that you have to save the world. Just *do the task allotted to you*, even if it is small. Every one of us is given something to do in life, and if that is done well, then you will find that the Light-force can function correctly within you, and that is more beneficial to the world than overdoing everything and collapsing. That doesn't help the Light circulation inside and outside you.

Dealing with Crisis

As already mentioned, this planet is going through a crisis, and being on the Spiritual Path does not mean you will be free from crisis in your life. Going through a crisis is not exceptional; it is just part of being human. What is important, however, is to *understand* the process. We will investigate what crisis means for you on a personal level, and then we will expand that to the level of society and the world. It is important to understand what is behind individual crises, because everybody has them. In fact, just being in this physical body is a crisis in itself!

Behind every crisis, whether it is personal or planetary, there are three things: *fear, insecurity* and *expectation*.

Most problems with personal relationships occur because of an expectation that the other person will be perfect. *You* don't have to be perfect, but the other person does! This can happen with parents, children, family, friends or work colleagues; expectation is a common cause of all kinds of relationship crises. You expect the other person to be something according to your ideas, and of course that is not who they are, therefore something is wrong in your relationship. If you are wise, you might end the relationship; otherwise you will struggle for many years. Alternatively, you can change yourself and change your expectations of the other person. When our expectation of a situation or relationship is not realized we commonly have a crisis.

Insecurity is another cause of crisis. You may have a job where the boss can dismiss you at any moment; or you may be insecure about whether your relationship is right for you; or perhaps you are unsure whether the spiritual path you are following is right for you, whether you should go to this teacher or that teacher, or whether you should change to something else. Insecurity is one of the prime causes of crisis. Another cause is fear. It may be physical fear or fear of a person. It may be the fear of change, of changing your job, your lifestyle or your relationship. The fear of change is very common. In summary, whatever so-called crisis you have, it is always based on fear, insecurity or expectation.

The question is: Who is afraid, insecure and having these expectations? *The ego.* The bigger the ego, the greater the fear, the insecurity and the expectation—and the greater the crisis. As you progress on the Spiritual Path there can actually be more crises, not fewer. If your ego becomes larger, your expectation of people and situations becomes greater, your fear and insecurity about people and situations become greater, so the crisis inside you becomes greater. Just because you are on the Spiritual Path does not necessarily mean that everything will be a bed of roses.

Furthermore, when you start on the Spiritual Path you are not free of your ego. The whole thing can be a play of the ego. If you join the Hare Krishnas, you will have your ego; if you join a Tibetan monastery, you will still have your ego. No matter where you are or who you are with, you will have a problem with your ego, and consequently you will have crises. You can extend this to your family and friends or to your workplace, where you may feel insecurity or unfulfilled expectations. You carry such things with you in every situation in your life and therefore you have crisis after crisis.

Understand that being in a crisis is not unique to you; it is a continual problem in most people's lives. Unless you have the right understanding you will continue to have crises due to the ego. Although a crisis obviously appears to be bad at the time, it only exists because we have an ego, and the ego is insecure and afraid and has expectations that are not met. To put it simply: reduce your ego, reduce your crises; increase your ego, increase your crises.

Crisis is Rebirth

Part of this understanding is that crisis itself can bring about a change or transformation that will lift you from a lower to a higher level of being—in other words, a rebirth. A crisis activates your hidden potential and talents and awakens you to a higher state of being. It is an opportunity for your Soul to bring out talents and abilities that are normally dormant within you. If you have a dull, routine, crystallized life, then there is no opportunity for your hidden potential or talents to be expressed. So understand that crisis is a positive thing. While you are having a crisis it may not be pleasant, but when you look back on it from a distance you will realize that it did activate some hidden potential or talent you never knew you had, some response from within that helped awaken you to a higher state of being.

The planet itself is in a process of rebirth, which means that people will have a lot of crises. Every individual has to go through the crisis of rebirth. With understanding, however, we can help people go through this process more easily. First understand and solve your own crisis. Then understand the crises of the people immediately around you, how they can interact to become a harmonious and functional group and, with the power of that unified energy, begin to help the world.

We come now to the *key* understanding of the whole problem of crisis. While you are living only as the personality you will always have crises. The personality is always outwardly bound because the personality belongs to *this* world, so naturally the personality has to deal with this world and this world naturally has many problems; in fact, it is just one big crisis! So, as the personality you are bound, but the Soul inside you is always free. The Soul is always in a state of Ecstasy, Joy, Light, Harmony, Goodness, Beauty and Love, while the personality is always struggling with the problems of this world. *The Soul is internally free but the personality is outwardly bound.*

For the average person there is no relationship between the personality and the Soul, so the obvious solution to your crisis is to move into Soul-Consciousness. When you return to Soul-Consciousness you will experience that eternal sense of Freedom, Love, Joy, Harmony, Bliss and Oneness. When you experience this higher aspect of yourself—whether spontaneously or in meditation or chanting—you will know it is your *real* nature, and when you return to the personality and look at your problem you will say, "Crisis? What crisis?" This is the solution.

If you are wise, you will realize that we cannot solve the problem of crisis by using drugs or by normal physical or sociological means. *The real Life* involves not *only* this Physical Plane. The real Life is a continuum of dimensions and situations in the Inner Worlds, so it doesn't work to base the resolution of crises on physical solutions. Rather, we need to teach and help people to raise themselves above the personality and become the Soul. In the experience of the Soul, life becomes a vast, expansive Ocean of Reality, and you know that even the worst crisis is trivial compared to that vast Ocean of Being which you eternally are.

You can then return from Soul-Consciousness with a completely different view of Reality and deal with the problem. Very often it ceases to be a problem, but if it is still a problem you will have greater *power* to deal with it. That larger view within will give you the solution to any particular crisis. Remember, all these problems are usually caused by the ego, but when you return from that larger view of Reality the ego has disappeared and you will be able to work out the problem, or it will cease to be a problem altogether.

As an example, suppose you are feeling insecure because you have no money and no job. Obviously this is very real for you. Even if you go into a higher state of consciousness the situation will not change, because it is part of the reality of this physical dimension. However, what does change for you when you come back down from that higher level of consciousness is the way you work out the solution. Beforehand you may have been tense and self-destructive, but when you come down from that consciousness you can see with a clearer understanding and act calmly. The problem is still there because the world is still there, but *the way you deal with the world will change.* You will become calm and accept the problem as a challenge without the negativity of fear, anger, violence or insecurity.

Remember, any crisis is good for you in one sense. Obviously it doesn't seem good for you when you are experiencing it—especially when you don't understand the cause of it—but when you do understand, you will see it as an opportunity for growth and transformation. You will understand that there is a solution to the crisis, that all you have to do is free yourself from the bondage of the personality and you are back in the Timeless, the Eternal—your real condition.

So try to understand these processes. If you manage to reduce your ego you will have fewer crises in your life. Earthquakes, tidal waves, loss of jobs, death or any other difficult situations will still happen—you cannot prevent them—but your whole inner Being will react differently, from the eternal Freedom of your Soul. Nothing that happens in this physical dimension can affect the Eternity of your Soul. This knowledge gives immense power within you: the power of Knowledge, of Realization, is fantastic! You know that this world is imperfect and that there will always be problems—that is just the law of this world—but when those problems come, you will be able to deal with them with an expanded understanding. And instead of being bound, you will always be free. ⚹

Finding True Happiness

THE SECRET OF ETERNAL LIFE

CHAPTER 2

"The way out of the struggle is to reconnect to your Source.
The Spiritual Path begins for you when you have a desire
to reconnect to that source. And then you are faced with
a dilemma: how do you reconnect to your Source?"

You may have been searching for Eternal Life, or some similar concept, all your life and you haven't found it because you haven't had the right approach so far. So I will try to explain this approach as much as possible in a few words, to help you experience Eternal Life *now*, because Eternal Life is not something you can buy, acquire or meditate for—it already *is*.

Man is Always Searching for Happiness

Ever since you were born you were searching for happiness. When you were a baby you were reaching out for your mother or father's hand because you wanted happiness. As a small child, you always thought that if you could get this or do that it would make you happy. Later when you bought your first car, you were happy for a while until you discovered that it cost you money to maintain it. As a student your parents may have encouraged you to study hard and become a top scholar, and when you achieved that goal you thought you would be happy. Again, you had the initial thrill but then you realized that after all that hard work and struggle you had to find a good job. After you found a good job you were happy for a short time until you realized all the problems associated with work.

Just think it through, item by item, situation by situation, the many times you thought that if you had this or that you would be happy. If you are honest with yourself you will realize that something inside you was always looking for that point of happiness, always thinking that if you had that *something* you would be happy. You may have had a little thrill for a while and then the satisfaction wore off and you wanted *something else*. Where was the lasting happiness?

People are searching for happiness all the time, but because the average human being at this level of evolution doesn't really understand what true happiness is, naturally he or she is trying to find this happiness in everything, everywhere. Obviously, seeking happiness itself is not a problem. The problem is *where* we are searching for happiness and *how* we are searching for happiness.

You first have to consider the real meaning of happiness and what it is you are seeking, because obviously you can search for happiness through thousands of material items, thousands of situations, thinking each time you will find lasting happiness and realizing each time that it isn't so. So the questions to ask yourself are: What is happiness? Am I searching in the right direction, in the right way, for happiness?

The Material Energy of the World

Everything that exists in the physical Universe, from the atom to the plants, animals, human beings, planets, solar systems and galaxies, is all part of the material energy. Your parents are material energy and everything in your environment is material energy, and so naturally you become part of the material energy. In other words, from the moment you are born you are swamped by material energy, or MĀYĀ (Sanskrit: usually translated as "illusion" or "delusion" but is simply the material energy of the Universe.)

So all this grabbing of material things is actually the result of your being directed by the material energy of the world. The material energy of the world, however, has nothing to do with who you really are; you are simply a victim of this energy, reacting to it and obeying it without realizing. Through the media and advertisements you are obeying the call of Māyā. So you spend a lot of time working hard so that you can have more and more objects, and because every object is an energy-field of material energy, you gather more of this energy towards you. You express yourself and search for happiness through that material energy in the form of people, objects and situations, and you think that is what life is about. You have become overwhelmed with the material energy of this world, and have completely forgotten who you are and where you have come from. You have forgotten that you are a nonmaterial being—a Living Soul, a spiritual entity, a radiant Being of Light existing also in the nonmaterial dimensions of Reality. Furthermore, you have also forgotten that you are only here on this planet on a temporary "holiday" because of your past actions—your KARMA.

For thousands of lives, you have been coming back into this world because you are always attracted to material objects, situations and people. This produces KARMA, and by the Law of Karma you have to work out the karma you have produced in the past. This continual circulating back into incarnation, life after life, is called Saṁsāra, or the Wheel of Birth and Death.

With each incarnation you produce more karma, which traps you further into this world, and because the world is not perfect you encounter pain and sorrow; you experience life as moments of happiness and moments of unhappiness. While your Soul[1] keeps incarnating, suffering and enjoying, incarnating, suffering and enjoying, you cannot make much progress on the Spiritual Path. (You remain what we call a *young Soul*, one that is under the influence of Māyā and keeps circulating on the Wheel of Saṁsāra.)

---

1 You don't *have* a Soul; you *are* the Soul. "The *individualised* Soul, JĪVA (in Sanskrit), takes on a personality, the recognizable human being, life after life, until it attains freedom in Nirvāṇa. In the East it is called the *Thinker* and the *Reincarnating Ego* because it takes on a new personality with each new incarnation. The Soul itself does not reincarnate. In one sense, *nothing* reincarnates, because the Soul never leaves its own realm. But, with each new life the Soul makes a new personality for itself *in the likeness of the previous one*. Only the shadows (the bodies of the personality complex) change, life after life."

From my book *Heavens & Hells of the Mind*, Vol.1, p. 35 (Sounding-Light Publishing, 2007)

There comes a crisis point, however, when you as the Soul begin to reflect on this situation and somehow your inner consciousness begins to know something is not right, that this is not how existence should be. We are talking here of existence, not one life, but a series of lives. Your Soul begins to wake up and in that lifetime comes the great moment when the real Journey begins.

The Way Out of the Struggle is to Reconnect to Your Source

The history of Humanity is one of continually struggling with matter, with this physical world. For hundreds of thousands of years human beings on this planet have wanted to change Nature, because we think that if we change Nature we will be totally blissful and attain our purpose in life. This is an illusion, and it has continued for thousands and thousands of years. We always think that this time we can conquer matter, this time we can travel through space and be gods of the Universe, but even the most far-fetched ideas of science fiction are still struggling with the matter of the physical world.

Once you realize that this struggle is futile, that you no longer need to struggle with Māyā, you have taken the first step towards finding what is really important: *the way out of the struggle.*

Don't take this as a philosophy because it isn't. It's the experience of thousands of people throughout the ages who have attained Higher Consciousness. Buddha would say the same thing if he were here: *The way out of the struggle is to reconnect to your Source.* What does this next stage of the Journey entail? What does it mean to reconnect to your Source?

Every living human being has a physical body, a temporary house, but we also have a source from which we have come, a divine source. The Spiritual Path begins for you when you have a desire to reconnect to that source. And then you are faced with a dilemma: *how* do you reconnect to your Source?

So you begin what we call the *seeking stage*. You listen to Hindu swamis or Tibetan monks; you go to a Christian church, a Jewish synagogue, a Muslim mosque. This is where the beginning of the Path is so confusing because the world offers so many choices and steers you in so many directions. With the ease of communication nowadays, you can search the Internet and get all kinds of information. Your mind can become overloaded with conflicting ideas from philosophers, theologians, metaphysicians and religious people. It doesn't mean that the Dalai Lama is wrong or the Pope is wrong. All it means is that out of that welter of confusion, you have to find *your* path, what *you* have to do to reconnect.

Here lies your dilemma and this is where you need a real Teacher, not someone who teaches theoretical ideas but who has actual experience, because the Spiritual Path is only experience. Some of the greatest saints had no philosophy or structured thinking whatsoever; they just *experienced* the inner realities and they taught from that. People were able to follow their instruction and experience the Inner Reality without any kind of background philosophy, without getting bogged down with complicated theological doctrines that lead precisely nowhere.

So I will try to simplify the whole issue from my personal experience so that you can understand what this spiritual quest, the search for Enlightenment, is really about. There are basically two paths to Enlightenment: the *Passive Path* and the *Active Path*.

The Passive Path

The Passive Path has been the favourite spiritual path for about six thousand years now, both in the East and the West. For the first four hundred years of Christianity, the Desert Fathers who went out into the desert to find solitude and silence followed the Passive Path, and it was followed by many Tibetan, Zen, Buddhist and Chinese schools. It is still popular today, especially in India, with the schools that follow the Way of the Heart.

The Christian Mystics and some Sufi and Zen schools still recommend the Passive Path, which means that wherever you are—in a monastery, in the desert, near a mountain or a lake or just by yourself at home—you seek *solitude* and *silence*. In other words, you cut yourself away from society, away from family, from work, from engagement in your environment, from engagement in Māyā, the great stream of material energy. You remove yourself from everything in order to find the God within you, not through active exercises or techniques like chanting mantras and complicated meditations but by *simply being still*.

The teachings of the ancient Tibetans, the early Christians and all the schools on the planet who followed the Passive Path, said, "Kill your desire, kill your thinking, kill your physical activity; be still and be quiet." This is because the Passive Path relies on quietening the activity of the body, quietening the activity of the emotions and quietening the activity of the mind, until there is a total stillness. In that stillness You, as the Living Soul, become alive, because previously all the busyness and activity of Māyā had been *preventing you from experiencing yourself as a Living Soul*. After a time you suddenly realize that *You* have always existed in that Stillness. The happiness you seek has always been there, and that which we call the *Secret of Eternal Life* has always been there; it is *you* who were not there.

So the whole idea of the Passive Path is to reduce all activity inside you so that as a Living Soul you can be born again, that is to say, realize that you are not a slave to the tremendous, fluctuating energies of Māyā. You realize the true Soul-Nature which you have always been, that which the activity of Māyā has been veiling. Remember, all the energies of your mind, emotions and your physical body are all part of Māyā, the material energy.

The Passive Path is still a valid path but it is becoming an increasingly difficult path to follow because of the immense activity of the planet. Stabilizing and ceasing all activity inside you or removing yourself from your environment is not something that really suits Westerners today. If you try to fully practise this path only, you will be totally out of tune with yourself, with your environment, with society and all your relationships. The Passive Path may have been fine in the olden days but it is not applicable to our society today because it will create great disharmony in your life if it is the only path you follow.

It's important to understand this aspect because it is very common amongst Westerners who are beginning their spiritual search to follow those teachings of the East that emphasize the Passive Path. Part of it can be applied, however, and in our School we use the Passive Path in proportion to the other path, the *Active Path.*

The Active Path

The Active Path relies on the power of Sound, in the form of mantras and divine names in different languages, to *purify* the surrounding energies of Māyā to such a degree that the higher vibrations of the spiritual realms can be sensed internally. Unlike the Passive Path, this path works with *activity* to elevate the energy-vibration of your whole personality structure until it is in tune with your Soul-Vibration. In other words, this Path involves activating the energies inside you to *transcend* Māyā.

Once again, it is important to use both the Active and the Passive Paths in proportion. If you use only the Active Path then, due to the already overactive Māyā structure within you and within the world, you will be out of balance with your family, your work and your environment. So the idea is to work with the two systems, the active and the passive, so that you always maintain a balance between your inner life and your outer life. Using only one path or the other is no longer applicable, or at least if you do you will have problems.

Now we come to another important detail. Within the Active Path, there are two kinds of meditation processes:

a. *Universal* (not based on race, culture or tradition).

b. *Conditioned* (based on race, culture or tradition).

The Universal Meditation Process

The beauty of this form of meditation is that every single man, woman and child on this planet can work with it because it is not conditioned by any race, culture, religion or environment. This process of meditation works with the techniques of *Breathing, Listening to the Inner Sound* and *Looking for the Inner Light*.

Everybody breathes so the breathing meditations are truly universal and based on life itself. (I don't mean the Haṭha Yoga breathing techniques here, as they are somewhat different.) You can be Russian, Chinese or Hungarian; you can be an atheist or a very religious person—it makes no difference. As a human being you breathe, so you can use *Breathing* techniques.

It is the same with the Inner Creative Sound (what the esoteric schools call the *Logos*, the Christians call the *Word* and the Hindus call

NĀDA or ŚABDA-BRAHMAN). The Divine Creative Word is resonating inside every human being right from birth, even before birth in the womb, so *Listening* techniques are unconditioned and have nothing to do with any belief system. And similarly, the Inner Light shines within everyone (in the Crown Chakra, slightly above the top of your head), regardless of what they believe in or don't believe in.

So the great thing about the universal or unconditioned techniques of active meditation is that anybody can use them. The Breath, the Sound and the Light are within you already, so you don't have to become a Christian, a Buddhist, a Taoist or a Tibetan monk. Just sit quietly and breathe, listen and look inside.

The other system of active meditation, the system most people generally follow, is that which is *conditioned*.

The Conditioned Meditation Process

The conditioned meditations consist of rituals, devotional singing, chanting and mantras. Most of these meditation processes come from traditions such as Tibetan Buddhism, Chinese Taoism or Hindu sects that worship KṚṢṆA (Krishna), RĀMA or ŚIVĀ (Shiva), for example, or from Christianity, Sūfism or Islam. Because they come from a religious tradition, therefore, you are usually required to be converted to a particular religion. There is nothing wrong with that but it's important to realize that you are going to become conditioned. But ask yourself this: "Do I want to be conditioned? Is it necessary for me to become a Zen Monk when the state of enlightenment is already here within me?"

People from the West often want to follow Eastern systems like Buddhism, Hinduism, Sūfism or Zen, because they think that by converting to that system they will attain Enlightenment or the knowledge they are seeking. They think that how they are in their present religion is not perfect, but joining some other tradition will make them perfect. But this is a mistaken belief. When you haphazardly go from one thing to another, because you think that the grass is greener on the other side, it means that you still haven't understood what you are really looking for. What you are looking for is already inside you.

Furthermore, every tradition is a partial expression of that religion and not the total reality. For instance, a Hindu swami only knows what a Hindu swami knows; a Japanese Zen Monk is only familiar with a particular Zen school, which may have originated from some other Buddhist tradition in China; and a Christian evangelical group may not give you the total meaning of Christianity but only a partial meaning, as expressed by that group. So now the question is, do you want to understand a particular religion only in a partial way, or do you want to understand its greater meaning?

In India it is quite common to be given only one MANTRA, and by working with it you transform your whole attention and consciousness into the particular energy-field of that mantra. That mantra can therefore liberate you along *that* energy-line, and no more. Similarly, a prayer is an energy system that works along a particular line of energy, and it can't work in any other way. So do you want to use one mantra and be enlightened along one particular line? Or do you want to remain open to the universal Divine Revelation? There is nothing wrong in working with just one particular energy-line, but you will feel its limitation.

In our school we teach a system that embraces all, and everything has its place. We chant mantras in Sanskrit, Hebrew, Latin and Arabic because we understand the power of those languages, not because we are limited by any tradition. We don't say that we only do this or that as part of the process of evolution or development. So in this way you can use mantras or even rituals of any tradition so long as you know that they help you along the way, but are not *the way*. With the right understanding, you can use a ritual to attain the state of consciousness whereby ritual is no longer needed. The tradition, ritual or technique is only there to get you to the state of Freedom, Self-Realisation or Enlightenment. Whatever you like to call it makes no difference—they are just words anyhow. The real inner experience is totally indescribable.

It helps to have a background understanding of what you are doing and why you are doing it, and so hopefully this clarifies some things for you. The key message I want to give you is that once you reach the point where you are no longer satisfied with life, when you realize that nothing in this humdrum life can give true and lasting happiness, then you do need a Spiritual Path. So with wisdom and the understanding of where all these systems come from, how they where created and why they were created, you can be intelligently aware of the direction of your chosen path. There is nothing wrong with any of these systems but you have to understand their purpose, and once you understand their purpose you go beyond the technique and you are there—Enlightenment, Eternal Life, is shining clear and bright within you. ✗

Why Meditate?

THE TRUE PURPOSE OF MEDITATION

CHAPTER 3

"The Kingdom of Heaven is within you already.
Nirvāṇa is within you already. All you need to do
is connect to It in a direct way. That is all."

Nowadays, most people have wrong ideas about spirituality, even those following the Eastern path. Many people practise yoga techniques purely for relaxation. For the past twenty or thirty years it has been taught in the Western world that when you are very busy and have a lot of stress in your life you should do some yoga exercises, breathing exercises, or "meditation" to relieve the stress. So people started doing all these exercises and meditations to relieve stress in their lives, which of course has nothing to do with meditation at all. To improve your health or relieve stress are not objectives of meditation. This is a modern idea, and a very wrong idea.

So I will tell you why people meditated in ancient days, going back to the ancient Egyptians, the Babylonians, the old Jewish civilization, the early Greeks and Romans, and the early Christians and Sūfīs. Why did they meditate? It was not for the reasons that most people in the West meditate today.

To understand the idea of meditation, we need to look at how a human being is made up and how the Universe is made up. Otherwise you won't understand why people should meditate. You will need to accept it as a theory at first, but later on you will discover it in meditation yourself as a truth.

You are Both a Soul and a Personality

Each of us is a *Living Soul,* existing in a radically different reality to this one. You, as a Living Soul, live in a Soul world. You can call it the Causal Worlds—very refined, high frequency, semi-Light, semi-material worlds. You live as a Living Soul in these worlds.

But you also have a personality that exists down here on this level. On this level you have a physical body, you have a mind, and you have emotions. Each of these—the physical body, the mind, and the emotions—have their own sphere of activity in and around you. You can see the physical aspect, but the mental and emotional vibrations you cannot see. If you become clairvoyant, of course, then you can see these things; but the average person is not clairvoyant, so the average person can only feel them. You can feel people's thoughts, you can feel people's emotions, and you can touch them physically, but all of this is only of the personality which lives in this world.

So you are both a Living Soul and a personality, and the problem arises because there is no conscious link between these two aspects of yourself. You don't remember yourself as a Living Soul; you know yourself only as a personality. In the education system, at home, and in church you are taught about your personality—about your body, feelings, moods, desires and thoughts—but you still cannot experience yourself as a Living Soul, as a spiritual entity apart from and beyond the personality. Therefore, you cannot experience the other Universe in which the Living Soul abides—a greater Universe, a radiant Light-Universe. (Refer to Endnote, page 244.)

In the East they use a different language to describe the same idea. They call the Soul ĀTMAN, the Spirit or the Self. They say that you have Ātman (Spirit), you have MANAS (the mind), you have KĀMA (the desire-nature), and you have the physical body.

Whether you follow an Eastern or a Western idea, however, the basic problem is that there is a disconnection between yourself as an immortal spiritual entity and the perishable self that exists in this world. Therefore, the Ancients made an effort to connect the two, so that while living in this world they became consciously immortal. *That connecting process is meditation.*

So the true purpose of meditation is to link yourself up within yourself. This is why the Easterners use the word YOGA. In the Hebrew tradition it is *Yichud*. Yoga does not mean exercise, it means *union*. Yoga is the uniting of that spiritual entity within you with the material entity which you observe yourself to be.

A Good Meditation is Very Simple

From the very beginning it is important to understand why you meditate. If you have a wrong idea of meditation, or if you meditate for the wrong purpose, then you will not attain that result which is the true purpose of meditation. This is why it is important also to choose the *right kind* of meditation. During the past six thousand years, people have forgotten the true idea of meditation and have devised intellectual exercises that actually take you *away* from that idea of union. The Buddhists, the Tibetans, and the Jesuits of the Christian tradition, for instance, invented very long, complicated, stressful visualizations and thinking processes and called them "meditation," and they thought that through those processes you could attain Higher Consciousness.

The problem, however, is that the more complicated the exercise, the less chance you have of succeeding. This is why we have to clarify what meditation actually is. A good meditation is very simple; it *has* to be simple, because a complex meditation will keep you tied to mental activity. The very complicated Buddhist and Christian forms of meditation keep the mind actively engaged in some visualization or thought-process, so you remain on that level. You (your consciousness) cannot move up or down and you cannot unite within, because you keep activating your mind. The whole idea of a good meditation is to quieten the mind, to make the mind completely *still*. And you have to understand very scientifically why that is so.

You have a physical body, you have an astral or emotional body and you have a mind body, and each has a different frequency of vibration.

Your physical body vibrates very slowly, your emotional body vibrates faster, and the mind body vibrates faster still. And then there is your Soul, which has a very rapid and fine vibration, and you cannot perceive it unless you cultivate that vibration. So you cannot ever perceive the Soul by simply remaining on the physical brain level, because the brain's rate of vibration is too slow. Nor can you perceive the Soul by feeling, because the emotional body is still too slow. Even by thinking, you cannot perceive the Soul, because your mind body is still too slow. Any meditation that continually over-stimulates your physical, emotional, or mental processes will develop only those levels of your personality; it will not connect you to the Soul level. So, to perceive yourself as a Living Soul, you have to go *beyond* physical, emotional, and mental processes.

The Soul Realizes that Something is Missing

Over thousands of years, people have invented two basic kinds of meditation process: one which connects you to yourself as a Living Soul, and the other which develops you horizontally (outwardly into the world), perhaps developing your emotional nature, or your mental faculty, or physical abilities, or psychic powers (SIDDHIS). But then the results are vastly different. Many of the Tibetan and early Haṭha Yoga forms of meditation, for instance, were invented to develop psychic powers, so that one could levitate, walk on water, go through fire, and so on. They thought that the purpose of meditation was to develop those powers. They had already forgotten the higher purpose of meditation, which is to *unite yourself as a Living Soul.*

If you were taught that you are only this personality, and you are content with such an image of yourself, and you cannot visualize yourself to be something deeper, then the idea of meditation will be meaningless. You will say to yourself, "I already am what I am! I already am a successful bank manager," or "I already am a multimillionaire!" You have a fixed idea of what you are, so there is no reason to be anything else. That is a limitation. It is why hundreds of millions of people never enter the spiritual life, never seek Union with the Absolute, never come to know themselves as living, immortal Souls. They are already satisfied with their image of themselves. They may be happy in whatever role they are in, and therefore they say, "This is all there is. I am quite happy as I am. Why should I meditate?" And that is fine, too.

However, there comes a time in everybody's existence, in the long life-cycle of the Soul, that no matter how successful you are in the world, you are still not happy. Even if you are the richest, most powerful, most influential person, you are still not happy inside. This is when the Soul realizes that something is missing. The personality is doing all these things in the world, but something is still missing! Then you become very restless inside. You start searching for something else, because the Soul inside you sends down little messages to the brain which say, "Go and find something better!" You pick up these little messages and they inspire you to look for something that makes your life more meaningful. This is a reaction of the personality to an impulse from the Soul within.

Then the real problem starts, because then you get side-tracked by so many options. There are so many things you can do! You can do Tibetan Yoga; you can do Buddhist Yoga; you can do Zen; you can do all kinds of things. You become very confused, because each school will present you with a different idea, and each school will say that if you practise that system, you will "attain." There are a lot of KUNDALINI schools too, which are worse, because Kuṇḍalinī will tie you down to the nature-energy, a tremendous psychic field of energy with tremendous powers and capabilities, but nevertheless, it will tie you down to Nature.

The Higher Purpose of Meditation

So you are offered all these different methods and systems from different sources, and it might take a long time before you ask: "What am I meditating for? Am I meditating just to get healthy? Am I meditating to get richer? Am I meditating to get psychic powers?" And there comes a time, when you have spent maybe several lives doing these things, when suddenly you realize: "Hey, what is the Soul? What is this Divine Being above the Soul? What is the nature of God? Is it better to seek psychic powers and be able to walk on water, or is it better to seek Divine Consciousness, the Absolute, an Eternal Reality?" After a while you become very sharp inside and realize that those other things are lower objectives. Then you begin to understand the true purpose of meditation.

You begin to look for sources that teach the higher, more noble idea of meditation, which is firstly to unite yourself with your Soul Nature, and then to unite the Soul Nature with the Divine Nature, so that in this lifetime you become *God-Conscious*.

God-Consciousness means being aware of Infinite Light, Infinite Mind, an Absolute, Boundless Sea of Existence, what the Buddhists call NIRVĀṆA. In the true, ancient sense of the word, NIRVĀṆA is an Absolute Field of Reality, an Unbounded, Limitless Existence, a World without bounds, a Universe without limits.

So you come to realize that the Path to that other world is through the process of meditation. Then you have to choose a system of meditation which is designed not so much to develop your personality (although that may be very useful), but rather to make a rapid connection to your Soul Nature, so that you become an immortal Living Soul.

This is already one evolutionary step ahead of Humanity. When you become aware of yourself as a Living Soul, able to function separately from your mental-emotional complex, that in itself is a huge leap in evolution. That is the first goal of Yoga, both Eastern and Western. In the Eastern Yoga schools they call this *Self-Realization*. In the Western system we call it "becoming a Living Soul." You realize that you can be without body, without mind, without emotions. There is a completely different being inside you, beyond time and space, beyond limitations, in a very happy and blissful condition. It is a totally blissful and boundless existence. And that is only the first stage—Ātma-Vidyā, or Self-Knowledge.

Then of course, after the Self-Realization process there comes the stage of *God-Realization*—Brahma-Vidyā or God-Knowledge—which is the uniting of your Soul with the Divine Nature. This is a further great evolutionary leap forward.

It is important to understand that Self-Realization and God-Realization can be attained *in this lifetime*. They are not just ideals to be attained at some future time, many lives from now. The whole purpose of meditation is to make you attain the first great leap of human evolution into Self-Realization, and then go even further and attain degrees of God-Realization. With this process you expand more and more into the Infinite Fields of Light that are already within us.

The Limitations of Human Perception

If a person thinks that what we see is the only world there is, that there are no invisible worlds, then of course, all these things are just abstract ideas. If there is nothing but this world, how can there be Worlds of Light?

We don't see the other worlds because the human vision is very restricted. In fact, what we see on the physical level is less than one percent of the Universe! Any scientist will tell you that the physical eye has a very limited range of seeing, and that the physical ear has a very limited range of hearing. Even the electromagnetic waves around us, such as radio and television waves, are still physical, yet even they are beyond the perception of the ordinary physical mechanism. Similarly, there is an even larger, nonphysical Universe all around us. There are the great psychic dimensions where people go after death, and beyond them are the Causal Universes, which are semi-Light, semi-material worlds. Beyond that are the lower Light Worlds, the intermediary Light Worlds, and the upper Light Worlds, vast Universes within and around us. And unless we understand the principle that these things exist, and then know that we have a process to attain them, we can never perceive them.

Philosophers have mentioned the possibility of the existence of other worlds, other dimensions, other realities. These remain just philosophical ideas. But we say that these things *do exist,* and that through the meditation process we can actually *experience* them. It is simply a case of tuning your mechanism to experience those invisible dimensions.

You have to understand the possibilities. You have to understand that you are living in a very limited world, that what you see is not all there is, that there are much *greater* possibilities.

Human beings are functioning at only one percent of their potential. Why? Because people don't even know that these greater realities exist! And if they do, it is only a theory of philosophy, metaphysics or theology. Students study these theories, and when they finish university they forget about them and get on with "real" living—making money! Making money has become the purpose of life for the millions.

But suppose you begin to realize: "What if the philosophers were correct? What if there really are such things? What if Nirvāṇa really exists? What if there really is a Kingdom of God? What if these things are true? Then what?" Then, of course, the logical question is: "How do we get there? What is the process, the method?" Then you come to that very disturbed stage, the *seeking* stage. You go to different talks and lectures, to different swamis, to different gurus, to different teachers, seeking the way. You ask questions, you try this, you try that. You try all kind of things, because something within you is impelling you to find out how to break through to those higher Realities. And you will not be satisfied until you actually do so, until one day you actually experience yourself as an entity beyond body, mind, and feelings, a completely separate entity living in a separate universe.

In this higher state of meditation, you realize that if your body dies, it makes no difference. If your mind stops functioning, it makes no difference. If your emotions cease, it makes no difference. Nothing here makes any difference; you continue as a living entity. That is the first major revelation inside you. Then comes a much deeper, much higher revelation: your connection with the Divine Nature, with the Universe, with higher Realities, unfolds degree by degree. The Revelation unfolds endlessly within you.

What Kind of Meditation?

So we have established that there is a reason to meditate. The next thing to consider is: what is the right kind of meditation for this purpose? Because there are specific meditation processes for specific purposes. If you want to develop psychic powers, you can do Kuṇḍalinī Yoga or Tibetan breathing exercises. Then you can become a master of *this* level of Creation, and for some people that is an ideal of meditation. But we say that it is a very limited ideal, because it will keep you in these lower realms. Through such processes you cannot cross the Great Divide out of the three lower worlds (the Physical, Astral, and Mental

Planes) into the Causal World and beyond. (Refer to the diagram *The Seven Great Planes of Being* at the front of this book.)

So you have to ask yourself: "Where do I want to go? What do I want to experience? What do I want to be?" Then you have to choose that kind of meditation process that will take you to your objective.

Modern seekers make the mistake of thinking that all meditation processes are the same, that they all lead to the same goal. They think that if we swing a pendulum, it is the same; if we go to a medium, it is the same; if we do Haṭha Yoga, it is the same; if we work with crystals, it is the same. But these things are *not* the same! Look! When you go to a railway station, not all trains go to the same place! It is a grave error of modern consciousness to try everything out because it is "all the same." Different processes have *vastly* different results. Obviously, if you want to know yourself as a Living Soul, you don't do exercises which lead you to psychic powers, because they will take you in a completely wrong direction for your purpose.

The right kind of meditation, however, is a scientific process that does lead to Divine Consciousness, to Nirvāṇa, to the Kingdom of God, to the Absolute Worlds of Light, to an Infinite Field of Mind. In this process of meditation you work with a mental formula, a mental-wave, using a sacred language. In the East you would be using Sanskrit, in the West you may be using Hebrew, both of which are sacred languages. It is not the language that is important, however, but the idea behind it. And the idea is that you use a mental-wave.

A mental-wave is like a structure of thought. It is a sound inside you, but a much more refined sound than a physical sound. You could listen to a physical instrument sounding a note, for instance, and that would be like meditation on an exterior level. The principle is the same: you listen to a sound, which is a formula, a frequency, a vibration. But we use a deeper device: the mind itself. It is natural for the mind to think. So, rather than using a physical sound, you are using a vibration or sound formula in the mind (a MANTRA).

The mental-waves vary according to a scientific principle. You begin to intone or announce the sounds in your mind and listen to them, just as you could make a musical sound physically and listen to it. But in meditation you are intoning a mental-wave in your mind, and then you listen to it. So the result is very much deeper. When you listen to sound on a physical level, the sound hits your ear and enters your brain, and you have an emotional response and then a mental response. But in meditation, rather than ending at the level of the mind, you begin with the mind itself and keep moving up. So the mind becomes the basis of your work. You start the meditation on the level of the mind, and then you rapidly move into Soul-Consciousness, because the Soul is the next level above the mind.

It is an amazing idea. You are bypassing the physical mechanism; you are bypassing the emotional mechanism; you are bypassing the thinking processes. You go directly to the source of the mind, and from there you jump right into your Soul Nature. So it is a very rapid process. Rather than struggling with exterior techniques for years and years, by working with the right kind of mental-wave you make rapid progress in meditation.

So you sit down and start using the mental-wave. You start using your mind to take you to the Kingdom of God. The mind can be a big problem, because it is always so active. But with this system you are telling the mind to be quiet in a way that suits it. It is very important to understand this meditation principle.

It is the Mind's Nature to be Active

When you do certain Raja Yoga exercises, or the Zen method, you have to force yourself to make your mind very quiet and still. But that is not necessary; it is a wrong method, because the mind's nature is to be active, and there is nothing wrong with the mind being active. So what you do is lead the mind along an activity which it likes. You give it a certain mental vibration, and because the mind is active, it works with it. But what the mind doesn't know at the time is that there is a trick in this, because that vibration will actually slow the mind down and make it very still and quiet. So, in the beginning the mind starts working with the vibration quite happily, and as it gets caught up with it, the mind becomes slower and quieter until finally it is stopped, without effort, without stress, without great force. *Then, when the mind stops, you become aware of yourself as a Living Soul.*

The only thing which stops this awareness is your mind. When you can make your mind quiet through meditation, then you realize that you are already in the Eternal Timeless Condition, but you normally have a vibration in your mind that veils your awareness of it.

Your Higher Reality, the Higher Light World, is a tremendous, bright vibration. But below it, your vibrating mind is like a great wall of a completely different frequency, so you cannot perceive your Higher Reality. When your mind becomes still and quiet, however, you perceive the Light World around you. You see the Light inside you and outside you. You are full of Light! The Light is shining everywhere, simply because the mind becomes still and quiet.

The problem has been that for many thousands of years people tried to *force* the mind to be quiet. Such techniques are not very productive because they work against the nature of the mind. The mind is allowed to be active but, because it is working with a very fine mental-wave, it becomes quieter and quieter in a very relaxed way, until suddenly the mind simply stops. Then you realize that you are transcending. You are going beyond the mind, beyond your personality. You are a timeless being, a Living Soul. It's as simple as that.

Meditation is based on the very simple truth that you already are a Living Soul. You don't have to make yourself be that; you *already are* that. It is simply a matter of realizing it, of coming to know it as a direct experience. The Kingdom of Heaven is within you already; Nirvāṇa is within you already. All you need to do is connect to It in a direct way. That is all.

Attaining Superhuman Evolution

When you become Soul-Conscious, you have taken the first step on the Path out of the human evolutionary stream onto a different evolutionary level. You are beginning in the lower rank of a *superhuman* evolutionary kingdom, another hierarchy of beings that already exists. Normally, people have to come to this level through aeons of evolution within the natural processes of nature, but at this time there is a possibility for human beings to consciously evolve out of the natural kingdom into the *superhuman* or *spiritual* kingdom by a conscious, willed effort. And that is the purpose of meditation.

Our purpose on this planet goes beyond just evolving out of the primitive stages to where we are now; that was only a small part of our evolution. *Our purpose on this planet is to attain the superhuman evolutionary level,* and the present human civilization has reached that intelligence whereby we can do it. If we make the conscious choice, and if we understand the goal and the process, we can enter the next evolutionary level. By the application of a particular knowledge and practice we can begin to grow out of the human kingdom into a superhuman kingdom.

When you experience your Soul Nature, your whole life radically changes. You feel that you are living in two universes: you are experiencing life here, while at the same time you are experiencing a completely different reality. And you realize that both are you! You are living in two worlds.

Later on, you will experience a still higher universe, a Divine Universe. Then you will be living simultaneously in *three* different universes. Then you will understand the dignity and the ultimate purpose of human evolution. When you have gone through this threefold evolution, you will realize: "Wow! People have forgotten this tremendous vision of why this planet was created, and why Humanity was put on this planet!" The actual purpose of Humanity is to live simultaneously in three vastly different universes—this part of Creation, the middle Creation, and the regions of Light—and thereby to bring these vastly different realities together. A perfect human being links these three realms in one entity, one being. That was the original plan for Humanity on this particular planet. It is a tremendous goal and a tremendous vision. As more people begin to realize this, the planet will change and, naturally, human consciousness will change.

We cannot change the planet through outer means. For thousands of years, politicians, sociologists, and religious leaders have been trying to change human consciousness by external means, by telling people to be "good," to love their neighbour, not to hurt people, not to kill, not to steal. Every religious leader has made rules about how people should live, and these ideas are very good, but people will never be able to live in such a way until they realize all these wonderful things about themselves and about the Universe. When they meditate and experience the tremendous inner happiness within themselves, and when they attain Divine Consciousness (which is a still higher level of meditation), then their whole lives change, even on the outer level. Then it becomes spontaneous and natural to do these things. When you realize that you are a Living Soul living in a very blissful condition, and that everybody else also lives in that condition, and that the whole Universe is filled with Love, then it is very easy to love others. It becomes your basic nature.

As more people do this, more people's lives will change. When the whole of society is doing this, then the life of the whole society will be totally different. People will naturally be good, and everything will blossom on this planet. Finally we will have peace on Earth. But until then there will be conflict and wars. While we have lost our essential connection with Reality, there is no way we can avoid this.

The Kingdom of God grows upon us. It becomes a reality for us when we become part of the Kingdom of God, and as more of us become part of the Kingdom of God, the Spirit will become an ever-greater power on this Earth.

There is no point in saying, "When I die I will go to the Kingdom of God." You won't. It is only through your internal recognition and attainment of Higher Reality while you are here in the body that you can enter the Kingdom of God.

We each must bring the Kingdom of God right down to this level, and so change nature and change society and everything else around us. The Kingdom of God is already here; what is missing is our connection to It and our conscious recognition of It. That is how simple it is, and that is why it is so difficult.

When you begin this path, then very rapidly you will develop some amazing insights and understanding about the true meaning of your existence on this level of Creation. At the moment you see one percent of Reality. Later on, when you become Soul-Conscious, you will begin to see ten percent of Reality. When you are God-Conscious, you will see one hundred percent of Reality. Then, of course, your whole vision of existence will be vastly different.

Psychic Powers Are But Side Effects

If meditation is not understood correctly, people will use it wrongly. Most people want to receive something to develop the personality, but this is not the purpose of meditation. When you begin to meditate, you will develop horizontally as well, because you will gain more knowledge and ability, and your inner powers will develop automatically. But these are not important; they are just side effects. What is important is that you move deeper and deeper into the Source of Reality.

This system of meditation has a completely different purpose to systems that were devised for developing psychic powers. We say that the development of psychic powers is not the major objective of Yoga. In fact, it is not the major objective of meditation at all. So, right from the beginning, you have to be clear in your mind that meditation has nothing to do with those systems that develop psychic power for its own sake. It is true that when you meditate deeply you very often develop certain abilities, but these are not the primary objective. Our objective is to go much deeper than that, beyond the nature realms, beyond the psychic dimension, into the Divine Realms, the Divinity Itself, Omniscience, Omnipresence, Omnipotence, the Absolute States of Consciousness. *That* is the real objective of meditation.

People have to be reminded over and over again of the glorious destiny of Humanity. There is a tremendous glory in human beings, and we have a great purpose on this planet, but people have forgotten. So first we remind them, and then we give them a suitable means for approaching that goal. Then, when people begin to practise it on a larger scale, it will uplift the whole planetary evolutionary field, because other velocities of existence will be introduced.

There is a Divine Mind working on a large scale that wants all of Humanity to attain to this condition. You are now at that point where you can register and understand it, and where you can do something about it. But realize that it isn't only for you, it is meant for a larger Reality. It is meant for the whole planet, for the Planetary Consciousness itself. You are part of a vast learning process stretching throughout all of Creation on this planet.

In the beginning, you think that you are meditating for yourself. You think you want to attain Nirvāṇa, the Kingdom of God, the Kingdom of Light, absolute Bliss or Happiness. But as you move along the Path, you realize that you cannot become enlightened for yourself. There is no way. You are part of a much larger process, a planetary process. You are meditating for Humanity. ✗

What You Need
For Your Journey
You Already Have
Within You

CHAPTER 4

"The Path is actually very simple; you already are the Path.
You don't have to go anywhere, you don't
have to become something else."

When we start our spiritual journey we often have the idea that we need to go from here to there, or we need to acquire something, therefore the journey seems to be an awfully long way. In all the great religions—in Buddhism and Hinduism, in the Jewish, Muslim and Christian religions, and in the Chinese and Japanese traditions—there is always mention of a journey or a path. When you use symbolism, such as going on a journey or travelling, then of course you have the idea that it is going to be a long process and that it will take a lot of hard work. This is how the religions and traditions made it appear to us, and this is why for the last few thousand years we thought of the Spiritual Path as some sort of arduous, difficult process—something like climbing Mount Everest with no food or water.

When you function from Higher Consciousness, you realize that what you need for your journey you already have within you. This is the great secret: that you are not actually going from point A to point B—the journey begins with you, and it *is* you. Where you are and what you are is already the Path; you are already on it. It is not a matter of thinking that you are going to attain something in fifty lifetimes and that you have to reincarnate a hundred times before you make your first step. The fact that you are in existence as a Human Being shows that you are already on the journey and that your very existence itself is the Path.

We have to switch our whole attitude towards the Path and have a more realistic understanding of it. It was fine for the people in ancient times to believe that it was going to take a long time, and that they had to develop all kinds of things, and go through many trials and tribulations. But in the New Age, in this Aquarian Age, we have to come to a more intelligent understanding of what this path is about.

The Path is actually very simple; you already are the Path. You do not have to go anywhere, you do not have to become something else.

However, this statement has to be understood properly because you can easily misapply it. For instance, you could say to a materialistic person that he is already the Path, that he does not need to go anywhere and that he is already complete. He will believe you quite happily, and because he is happy just being in a limited condition he will see no need to start on the Spiritual Path.

You Already Are What You Are Seeking

First, let us understand what we are already. We are embodied Human Beings; we already are that, from the lowest to the highest possible Divinity, the MONAD. We have a physical body and an etheric-vital body; we have an astral body, a mental body, and a causal body; and beyond that we are a triune, threefold Spiritual Self—ĀTMA-BUDDHI-MANAS. Beyond that we are the One, Indivisible Monad, which is also threefold within Its own essence. (Refer to the diagram *The Seven Great Planes of Being*.) This is the Path; we already are that. There is nothing that we have to attain to, nothing that we have to become. By constitution—by how we are as Human Beings—we already are it.

This is the first basic understanding of Illumination: you already are the Buddha, you already are the Christ, you already are Lao Tzu, or the greatest Saint or Master. The only difference is that these people actually realized this. It is not that they were different from us, but that they all realized what they really were. That is the big difference.

When Buddha or Jesus started off on the journey—or Moses or Mohammed, or any of the Great Ones who shaped and changed the world—they started off with a personality, complete with human frailties and human emotions. They started off with their own religious backgrounds just as other people did, and they thought according to the way society thought in those days. However, the difference was that they began to realize, through some process, that they were actually more than that temporary personal expression and that the personality is only an expression of these lower dimensions. They had higher realizations that there are subtle regions, within us and within the Cosmos, that are unbelievably different and more divine than this physical world. They began to sense themselves as Living Souls, beyond Time and Space.

They didn't do anything to put something more into themselves, nor did they have to acquire anything externally; it was simply an inner realization of what they were and a matter of *being* what they were. That is all it is: just this little trick of knowing or not knowing. Those who are enlightened know, while those who are unenlightened don't know, but they are basically the same people with the same possibilities—there is no difference.

If you have this idea that you have to go from here to Tibet, or from here to an Indian ashram to become enlightened, then you are not understanding the process. You do not have to go from any point to anywhere, because you are already complete and you are whatever you want to be. It's a matter of learning how to switch from your physical-body awareness, and your complete personal or ego awareness, to the complete causal awareness—that awareness of yourself as a reincarnating Soul in your causal body.

Beyond that, you have to flick into a deeper awareness of yourself as even more than a living Immortal Soul; that you are existing in pure and formless dimensions in the Buddhic and Nirvānic Worlds. And then there is a deeper, inward realization that you are the living, bright Monad, the Blazing Glory, the Absolute Glory of Divinity Itself. Wherever you are, in whatever space-time condition, you have to turn your attention more and more inward until you realize what you are. That's all. It's as simple as that. The sooner you learn the trick of moving inside to perceive the deeper layers, the sooner you become enlightened (or come to the point of Enlightenment) and identify with the higher aspect of Reality.

This Teaching is so important today because there are still the old schools of the Piscean Age (the past two thousand years) teaching the message that it will take many lifetimes to attain, because that was how they thought in those days. But if you rightly understand what you really are, then you know that it is not a matter of a journey in time on a horizontal level; it's rather a matter of refocusing your attention deeper and deeper inside yourself to *know* and *experience* what you already are, and that is all. This is the new Revelation, the new Philosophy of Enlightenment—the true Aquarian New Age.

Why Are We Not Experiencing What We Already Are?

On the physical level, our tasting, seeing, hearing, touching and feeling senses are actually outer expressions of inner senses; we also have those senses on the astral and mental levels, but they are more vast and complete. We also have them on the Soul-level, where every taste, every touch and every sight is infinite. Again, we have those senses inside us already. So what is the problem? Why do people not experience the Inner Worlds? If everybody has all these senses within themselves, why are they not walking Buddhas and Christs? Why is everybody not enlightened and experiencing what they already are?

So far as the great Universal Life is arranged within us, the energies are focused towards this physical world, towards the physical body. This is not just unique to you, but affects all life: the Human Kingdom, the Animal Kingdom, the Vegetable Kingdom, the Mineral Kingdom and the planet Earth itself. You are simply part of that great Cosmic

Energy that is focusing into the physical dimension. Our Planetary Evolution is proceeding through the Universal Life-Force focusing into manifestation, into the matter of the lowest and densest plane, the Physical Plane.

That is why the great Saints and Masters of India call this KALI YUGA, "the Age of Darkness", or the age of dense, material expression. *Kali* means "the dark" or "night", and it also means physical or material expression. We have reached the "nadir", the lowest point where Kali Yuga can function. After this there can only be upward movement. When you make a circle, you start from the top and you can only go down. By the very law of the circle, it can only go down to a certain point; after that it has to return to its source. It cannot keep going down, otherwise it is not a circle. The normal evolutionary process is driving towards and into the physical dimension, and this is fine in terms of the great cosmic clock of Evolution on this planet Earth. So we as human beings have reached our densest manifestation as expressed in this human physical body.

What this means is that because the evolutionary forces are concentrating on the unfoldment and development of the Physical Plane, naturally the consciousness of the people is physical. It cannot be anything else. This is exactly the reason why billions of people are not sensing themselves as Living Souls, or even as reincarnating entities. *Human beings are so totally focused on the physical level that their conscious awareness is only in the physical body and they cannot relate to anything that is not physical.*

In the same way, the animals cannot conceive of things other than just the physical; they do sense etheric and astral forces in life but, like humans, they mainly function on the physical. The plants also function on the physical; they *sense* but they are not consciously aware. Hence we are right in the depths of physical matter and we understand that this is normal, there is nothing wrong with it; it's natural and that is how it is. But then, if we want to step on the Path, the first key is to realize that we are already *it*; we are already that sevenfold Human Being (able to exist simultaneously on seven Planes of Being).

Obviously then, the Path is a shifting of your attention away from this physical world and into your total personal being, the personal ego or "I". And then the next stage is to shift from that personal ego into yourself as a Reincarnating Soul, as the Living Soul in your causal body. There you will be able to see your many lives, with a vast history of experience that you can call into your Being, to help with your understanding and intelligence. Then you focus further inside as a Living Soul beyond Time and Space altogether, existing totally in formless dimensions, and then beyond that to the Divinity itself, the bright Godhead which is you and which is God Himself.

So if we understand that the Path exists not so much as a journey but as a further *unveiling* of what we already are within ourselves, then rather than thinking of all the things we have to do, we need to think of all the things we *don't* have to do—and this is where the trick lies.

Here is an analogy: At night-time, your room is dark, right? When you go into your room, you don't have to chase the darkness out of your room. You don't have to get a broom and shovel and try to get the darkness out of the window or out of the door. All you do is switch on the light, and when you switch on the light the darkness just disappears. Translating that into practical terms, what we have to do is not so much accumulate many things within ourselves, but remove the obstacles, remove those things which prevent us from seeing and knowing ourselves as who we are. That is all.

The Obstructions to Enlightenment

Although every human being has the potential to reach higher levels of consciousness, we all have obstacles or blockages. The main blockages are the physical body, the astral or emotional body, and the mental body or mind. These are the three well-known obstructions to the possibility of Enlightenment.

In real life we are not all equal; some of us make more effort and some of us have more talents, more skills, and so on. So rather than having a universal rule for how everyone should go about reaching Enlightenment, you just have to look within and know what the obstructions are within yourself. Whatever you know is an obstruction within you, try your best to remove it.

Firstly, it could be physical; you could be so physical in your attention that the only thing you can see is physical life. Millions of people are like that—they are just totally physical in their focus and awareness. That is the biggest obstruction to attaining Enlightenment in their lives. So if they want to ever step on the Path, they have to think about that obstruction and do something about it.

Others are very emotional and the emotional body is their biggest obstruction. In certain parts of the world, people tend to react to everything in a totally, emotional way; they don't use any mind whatsoever, but immediately explode in emotional hysteria. If those people want to go on the Path, then they need to look at that instantaneous hysteria and uncontrolled emotion. That in itself is blocking the Realization of the Truth.

Then you have the other type of human being: the mental type, those who are always up in their heads and have minds like computers. You can see them programming everything they experience into "the computer" and they assess everything mentally. Now, that may be okay when you are dealing with physical life or when you have a job that requires that mental ability—that's fine. But in terms of attaining Self-Realization or Enlightenment, that computer-mind has to go! It is limiting the possibility of reaching Enlightenment. That is why using a technique of meditation that is based on endlessly thinking about something, is actually the wrong process. All you are doing is making the mental body larger by thinking about all kinds of things, and this in itself develops the mental body tremendously. You can be thinking about hundreds of things, but this does not quieten the mental body. The mental body, your thinking process, becomes the obstruction in the process of Enlightenment.

If you want to expand yourself as a Living Soul, you have to go beyond the mental body. There is no other way, because the mental body is still part of your personality. Above that is your causal body, and above that is You—the Boundless, Universal, Formless, Light-Being that you are. So if you have philosophies where you are endlessly thinking about something, all you are doing is developing yourself mentally, and consequently you are not able to go beyond that. So we are trying to give you a new way of looking at the Spiritual Path, as not so much a gathering of things, but *a removal of things.*

If you want to attain in this lifetime, you have to look at yourself and see where the obstruction is and what you can do about it. It may be that you have all three obstructions; then you really have a hard time! Some people can be emotional and mental, or emotional and physical, but on the whole, most people are either very physical or very emotional or very mental, and those are the three categories of human beings.

Remember, we are not talking about everyday, physical life here. I am not saying that you are not going to use your mind anymore, or feel anymore, or use your physical body anymore. Those things are all fine in your everyday life. Instead, I am talking about things you need to do to come to the point of Enlightenment inside yourself. It is also important to realize that there is nothing *wrong*; you don't sit down and start blaming yourself. It is simply a knowing about yourself, knowing that that is how you are and that's fine. A blockage remains a blockage until you recognize it as such. Once you recognize it, then you can do something about it.

Removing the Obstructions in the Moment Itself

Whatever your meditation process—whether you use a mantra,[2] or whether you use chanting or breathing techniques, or whether you use action as in the Warrior Schools—you have to realize your limitation and allow it to disappear in the moment itself. Whatever you *do*, the key to it is to dissolve yourself in that moment, to overcome the limitations you have in that moment, and it can only be done in that moment.

In the olden days, you sat down to meditate and were told that if you recite this or that mantra two and a half million times, then by that time you would reach Self Realization (and perhaps you did). You were looking at the Path as moving ahead: from the past, to the present and into the future. We don't do that. We don't say, "I'm sitting and doing this meditation technique because in a few years time I'm going to attain Enlightenment," because then you are journeying forward on this infinite and illusionary timescale. Instead, you sit there and simply

---

2 When you use a *mantra* (a sound sequence or Word of Power used in inward meditation to suspend the mental processes and connect to higher levels of Consciousness), you focus your attention deeper inside yourself to give you a moment of Enlightenment, or a *vision* or experience of the higher part of yourself. *That is Enlightenment.* Once you penetrate beyond your personality structure, once you even develop Causal Consciousness—where you know your past, present and future—then you will understand the flow of life and why you are as you are. Causal Consciousness is the first and lowest level of Enlightenment.

wipe away the resistance or the limitation you have, because in that instant, in that singular moment, *is* Enlightenment.

If you move your mind away from the sense of a timescale within you and just live that very second, that very moment, then you realize that that moment is an Eternity, that moment is an Infinity, that moment is Timeless, and it is the All. That moment *is* the moment of Enlightenment.

It is a matter of shifting your attention: from thinking about attaining something in the future, to actually *being* in the moment. And being in the moment simply means to go beyond your particular limitation, whatever it is, and jumping over it into the Eternal Moment.

This is the new, enlightened way of practising the Spiritual Path in this coming Age. It is learning to be more and more in the moment, because whatever you do in that moment is the key to Enlightenment. If you are using a mantra, it will be your key to Enlightenment. If you do a Warrior technique or a breathing technique, it will be your key to Enlightenment. When you say your mantra or do some action, you say it or do it in the state of Enlightenment. The mantra (or your way of action), the moment of Enlightenment and Eternity become synonymous.

I know it may be difficult to comprehend this, because we are all used to this old-fashioned Piscean teaching that it will take aeons of time to get there. But as I said, because you already *are* how you are constitutionally, you already have that *inside* you. Therefore you don't have to go on trying to get it for the next fifty lifetimes. All you have to do is remove what is preventing you from experiencing it.

To begin with, you have to think, "Why am I not experiencing myself as an integrated personality? Why am I disunited within myself?" The fields of psychology and psychiatry have been dealing with this for almost a hundred years. They have tried to figure out how this personality works and why it is disintegrated, and what to do about it. And that is only on the lowest level; integrating your personality is only the beginning of the great inward journey of Internal Revelation. Even on that level, you just sit down and be still. In that Stillness you are integrating your personality straight away.

A lot of new-agers devise all kinds of complicated techniques for integrating the personality by using a lot of mental stuff, when all they have to do is drop all that mental stuff—not develop it but drop it—and become still. In the moment of Stillness the personality will become integrated. It's very simple. They are doing it the wrong way; they're making it a big task instead of a simple task.

When you do your mantra meditation, if you say the mantra with a totally integrated personality it will be bright and clear and will immediately affect you. If you say the mantra when your physical body is not in harmony, or when your astral body is out of tune and your mind is going all over the place, then the mantra sound is not going to be clear at all. It will not have that power to enlighten you, that power to awaken you into unification with your Higher Nature.

Similarly, when you are working with a real, live, sharp sword, it teaches you in one movement whether you are an integrated personality, or an integrated Soul *and* personality, or a totally integrated Master. Because when you move your sword, when you are one hundred percent precise in its movement, it sings. This is the amazing miracle: it makes a swishing sound that is absolutely clear because you make that movement in perfect harmony with your own Self-Nature within, and you make it in perfect harmony with the environment. Now, if you are just slightly disorganized within yourself, if on the physical, emotional and mental levels you are not one hundred percent tuned-in—to the environment and to your Soul—then that sound is not there. You can practise it over and over again and each time you know whether you are in a perfect state or not in a perfect state.

So look at yourself, at least during the time of your meditation or devotional practice, during the time when you are doing your spiritual training or exercise. Find out what your hindrances are and remove the obstacles as best you can. If it is a physical-body problem, or you are in physical pain, try to make the body more comfortable. If it is an emotional thing, try to calm your emotions. If your mind is too busy, calm your mind by realizing that the busyness of your mind is a hindering factor. Remove the obstacles as much as you can, and then merge into the moment through the technique you are using at that time. In that moment is the Timeless Dimension where everything miraculously takes place in the Cosmos, and your Enlightenment is part of the miracle of the Cosmos.

Obviously, each of us has a different path to follow, in the sense that we each have to look into our own life-stream and ask, "What do I need to eliminate in my process of meditation, or what do I need to eliminate in my life, which would help bring about that moment of Enlightenment?"

Unfortunately, you have to work for your Enlightenment; the cleaning lady won't do it for you! It would be nice if you could just ring up the corner shop and say, "I want two degrees of Enlightenment, thank you!" There are some New Age teachers who say that you can achieve it in five minutes or ten easy lessons—well, forget them because they are fake. You cannot do that in one easy lesson, unless you are already at the moment of Enlightenment. There is such a thing as momentary Enlightenment, but only after you have already done a lot of work in raising the vibration of your physical, emotional and mental bodies—not when you just start off or when you come in off the street and take a course in Enlightenment. It does not work that way.

So, sometime in your busy schedule, just sit down and think about your possible hindrances, and realize that the Path is not that far away. It is exactly where you are. It is right in your breathing process, your thinking process, your feeling process and your activity. Even the simplest movement can produce Enlightenment—provided you are right there, in that moment, free of those physical, emotional and mental obstacles. Then whatever you do at that moment becomes your moment of Enlightenment, that *vision* or experience of the higher part of yourself. That's how simple it is. This will be the future teaching, or at least the new teaching for the process of Enlightenment in the New Age.

Help Others Towards Enlightenment

There is one more thing about the Spiritual Path that I would like to mention. In the past few thousand years, people were often selfish and thought only of their own Enlightenment, their own Self-Realization. They did it for themselves because they thought it was a good thing to do (and it was). In this New Age, however, your Enlightenment is not just for you alone. Now we need to think of what we can do for the total Humanity, for everybody on the planet, not just for *ourselves*.

Students on the Path don't understand how important this is. When you receive something, you have it for yourself, you are happy with it and that's fine, but you don't realize there are millions of other people who have no chance of receiving this teaching. If you had Cosmic Consciousness you would curl up in pain at the thought that, while all this amazing knowledge is available, there are millions of people in China or Vietnam or Latin America, for example, who will never have it because there is no translation, or because there is no possibility for them to have access to it.

If you help to enlighten another person, you are also helping yourself because that other person is yourself. You realize that the other person is looking through *your eyes* to you, and when you help to enlighten that person you feel joyous because you know that a part of you also has become enlightened. Each one of us is part of the universal Humankind, the one Human Archetype that must eventually come to Perfection.

So you start with yourself—naturally you have to—but then you expand and embrace more and more people so you can help them into the Stream of Enlightenment. Just one little thing can help them into the Stream whereby the Enlightenment Process begins within them. If you can be aware of this then your whole life will become more meaningful and purposeful.

The Mystery of Death

A ROAD MAP FOR YOUR
JOURNEY BETWEEN LIVES

CHAPTER 5

"There is no Being or God on the other side who punishes you in any way, who says you were bad so you go down, or you were good so you go up. It is just the Law of Universal Nature at work. After death you are automatically attracted to the condition that matches your vibration."

Reincarnation as a Universal Doctrine

In order to understand life we need to understand death. To understand both we need to have a foundation of knowledge, and it is this knowledge that is missing from our materialistic society. Death is not a subject taught in standard educational curriculums. Even most religious teachers don't know much about it. They may tell you what they believe in or what their traditional belief system says about it, without any experience or real facts about the mystery of death.

It is an amazing, wonderful and miraculous fact that we are multidimensional Beings living in a multidimensional Universe, a multidimensional Reality. The world around us is much more than what is only perceived by the physical senses. *We are more than just a physical body*. This is not a philosophy or theory—it is the foundation. Once this is explained, the idea of moving in and out of incarnation and the Law of Karma (action and reaction) will make total sense. Time and Space will make sense and Eternity will make sense.

This Teaching, that you existed before you were born into a physical body, has been known to all the ancient religions and has been taught as a universal doctrine since time immemorial. It was taught to the ancient Jews, and in the first three centuries of Christianity. The understanding of the Soul's existence before birth, that it comes back over and over again, was normal in the minds of the masses. It was a common belief, even in the old Jewish religion, that there is a past, present and future life, that there is an eternal continuum of the Soul and the Soul keeps coming back to gain experience. For instance, Jewish prophets of the past were expected to return, so when Jesus started preaching He was often asked questions like "Are you Elias who came back?" (Luke 9: 18–19) It was a popular idea that people "come back", or in other words, reincarnate.

In Christianity this was regarded as quite normal until the fourth century, when the church became part of the Roman Empire, ruled by materialistic emperors with a totally materialistic orientation. The church held a council and banned what they called "anathema", including the idea of reincarnation, the preexistence of the Soul, and many other things that were understood as normal in those days. They finally came up with what we know nowadays as Christianity, or the limited beliefs and ideas of Christianity, because it is extremely limited compared to what it was in the first three centuries. The ideas of reincarnation and the progress of the Soul after death have been lost to Christianity, and today Christians say there is no reincarnation, no preexistence of the Soul. It has been a false religion from the fourth century onwards.

Many religions, including Buddhism, Hinduism, the ancient Chinese religions and the Sikh religion, accepted the idea that you lived before, you live now and you live after. That was, and still is, common in those religions. But even in those religions that banned the doctrine, such as the Christian and the Muslim religions, it secretly survived. In the case of the Muslims, the Sūfis secretly taught it, and of course the Christian mystics, such as the Gnostics and the esoteric Christian schools, also taught it. So let's assume that, despite the aberrations of some religions that banned the idea, you understand that you existed *before* you were born into this physical body.

The Fall of Mankind

At the beginning of Creation—actually a little later than the beginning of Creation, a few hundred million years ago—you existed as a Living Soul. Imagine yourself as a Living Soul in the Causal World, absolutely radiant, blissed out and happy all the time. You live in a wonderful causal body, or *Radiant Body*, and you will continue to exist in that wonderful Radiant Body of yours for a very long time. You would not believe how beautiful you really are as a Living Soul!

As a Living Soul you are beyond time and space conditions, beyond the limitations of material existence, and it is you as a Living Soul that decides (and has decided many times) to incarnate into this world to gain experience. There was originally a group-decision by all of us (the Human Hierarchy of this planet) to incarnate and descend into the depths of the material existence of this physical world, and from then on we were provided with various bodies or vehicles.

Initially the *causal body* was given to us by the Solar Angels, who work within the aura of the Sun. Then the *Sons of Mind*, the MĀNASAPUTRAS, who work with the Mental Aspect of the Deity, gave us the *mental body*—a subtle, semi-Light, semi-material body which they formulated for us over several aeons. Another hierarchy, called the "Lunar Lords", then gave us the *astral body*, the feeling body, fashioning it over a long period of time from the forces of the Moon. Then another hierarchy, certain angelic types who work with Light-Substance, gave us the *etheric-physical body*. And finally, from the Animal Kingdom we inherited the *physical body*.

From this background, you need to know that your existence is actually part of a cosmic structure, extending over vast aeons of time. I am describing the incarnation process first so you have a greater understanding of where death fits into the overall flow of life. Once you understand the larger picture, the whole mystery of life and death will be put into perspective.

So we first began to descend from the Causal World as thinking entities in our mental bodies. Then we incarnated in our astral bodies as feeling entities, feeling through the astral substance of the Astral World. Then we descended into etheric-physical bodies and we began to function on the etheric-physical dimensions of our world. Finally, in the early days of the evolution of the planet we came down to the dense Physical World, where there was a problem: there were no corresponding human bodies available that would really suit the human beings that we are—*human* beings with majestic power and potential. On all the inner dimensions we were given the right vehicles, but there was no hierarchy that could provide us with physical bodies, so it was decided that we would use the bodies of the physical evolution of the day: the highest life forms of the Animal Kingdom that were evolving at that time. Originally we were not meant to be working in this animal structure in the Physical World, but there was no other alternative; otherwise we would still be functioning no lower than the etheric part of the Physical World. This is why the scientists say that we descended from the apes; we still have the animal impulses belonging to the Animal Kingdom that were inherited on the physical level.

So that was a big step, the so-called *Fall of Mankind*, because we descended from a human state into an animal state—on the physical level only. As soon as you leave the physical body, however, you realize that you are very different from the Animal Kingdom. You know this before you are born and also right after death. You know for yourself what makes a human being a human being, and what makes an animal an animal. There is no correlation between the two; they are different kingdoms altogether. In the Inner Worlds you know that, but while you are in this physical world you do not know.

The Soul's Decision to Incarnate

It has to be understood that your process of incarnation *starts* on the causal level long before you are physically born. In your causal body, together with another spiritual hierarchy of Angels, the *Karmic Lords* (those who deal with the working out of karmas and destinies), you as a Living Soul work out a system of energy-lines (Karma) that you need to work through in the next life. It is because you have made that decision that the incarnation process begins.

As a Living Soul, in your Radiant Body in the Causal World, you know exactly who you are and what you are, without the slightest doubt. You already know what your future life is going to be and what you want to achieve. Then you start coming down, firstly with the help of the hierarchies that created the mental body for us. They start reformulating your mind-body as it was in your last life—that is, with the same impressions, thought-patterns and mental vibrations. They give those back to you just as they were after your last incarnation. That takes time, so you spend a certain period in the Mental World. Then the next hierarchy helps you to build your emotional (astral) body exactly the same as it was last time, because the Law requires that you retain what you had previously. Then the same process happens for your etheric-physical body, and finally you find the people who will be your parents and will give you a physical body.

The physical body you inherit from your mother and father *is the only thing that is not you!* All the rest of your bodies are you—your etheric body, your astral body and your mind-body are really you, as you expressed yourself previously. It is the physical body that is different to that of the last life. When you inherit the physical body, you inherit some of the racial tendencies and physical features of your parents, but the feeling, thinking you is still the real you, although you begin to adapt yourself to your environment and to the family, race or culture you are born into.

A Sense of Limitation

While you are incarnating, your conscious connection with your Soul is *decreasing*. Here is the problem of life! Although as a Living Soul in the Causal World you are fully aware of your past, present and future, once you are enclosed in your mental body you lose the first connection with your Soul-Nature. You are living as an intelligent, thinking being, but you have little idea what you are living for or what the plan is. When you come down to the Astral World, another layer is put upon your Soul-Light and you are living as a thinking, feeling being, but you have further lost the plan. And then finally you come into physical incarnation and, as you know, when you are born you have totally lost the plan and from then on you are trying to find out what it is!

Each step of the incarnation process takes you one degree further away from the Light of your Soul. As you come down you are losing touch with your Soul-Awareness. It is like veil upon veil shrouding a candle flame until you can vaguely see it. I am talking here about the hundreds of millions of normal people, not the exceptions such as the Adepts, the Mystics or the Saints. As the mass of people incarnate, they lose touch with the original plan, the Soul-Intelligence within themselves.

At the time your mother becomes impregnated there is a moment when you as a Living Soul connect to the first cell by a slight Light-thread. As a Living Soul you feel it as an impact point and you know that your physical vehicle is about to grow and you have finally descended to the physical dimension. When the embryo has grown for about three or four months, you as a Living Soul have a stronger realization that you are about to incarnate physically. At the age of nine months, when you are physically born, there is of course a deeper impact on your Soul that you have landed on the Physical Plane, or rather that you have sunk to the depths of matter. In other words, you begin to sense the compression and limitation of having a physical body, which is totally unlike the freedom you experience as a Living Soul.

As a Soul you are limitless: your natural state is all-pervasive and your Intelligence extends to the depths of Space without any sense of limitation. Once you are physically born, however, your Soul begins to be aware of a sense of immense frustration from touching this dimension. There is no way you can compare your Soul-Consciousness and your physical-body consciousness; one is limitless and the other is totally limited. Why do you think that the first reaction of the baby is often to scream, "Waaa!" (Get me out of here! Why am I here?) It is then that you suddenly realize you have become trapped, that a tremendous limitation in consciousness has taken place.

As the physical body grows towards maturity, the Soul puts more and more energy and attention into it. These days, because people are extremely materialistic, there are children who are very familiar and comfortable with physical plane existence from an early age. This shows that human consciousness is becoming more materialistic, that the Souls somehow descend further and establish themselves more quickly into physical life in the Physical World. This is due to the incredible downflow of materialistic energies into the planet at this time, causing people to become more rapidly materialistic and focused in the awareness of the physical body, the furthest point of incarnation of the Soul.

The Soul's Plan

How long we live in the physical body, was originally envisaged by the Soul. The Soul already knows that it is going to live for only five days, five years, ten years or a hundred years, because the Soul has worked it out in the Causal World, in its own particular domain. But when you come down here a problem arises because society and relatives can interfere in that process, completely unaware of your Soul Plan.

It may be that you as a Soul decided you will live for only six years in the physical body to offset a complicated set of karmas from previous lifetimes. Then along come your parents, and all of society, who naturally do everything possible to prolong your life completely contrary to the wishes of the Soul. Your life might be prolonged, but upon returning from this life cycle the Soul says, "Oh no, now I have to redo the whole thing again; I have to go back next time for six years because I didn't do it this time." People find it very difficult to understand that each of us has a proper destiny. If you could truly understand it and follow it through, everything would be fine. But it is often messed up because there are so many interferences—from society, from parents, from religious authorities, and so on.

Some people who are more evolved actually know when they will die. The Yogīs, Saints and people who are tuned in to the Soul level know precisely that they are going to live a long life or a short life, and they even know how they are going to die. Jesus had already decided that He was going to live a short life; He died at the age of thirty-three. He didn't need to die at that time, but before incarnation He decided to do a quick work, a major reshuffle of the planetary energies, then to go out and have better experiences in another place. The Buddha lived to ninety years of age. He had already decided before incarnating that He was going to spend forty or forty-five years of His life teaching the masses, and He lived according to that particular length of time that the Soul decided.

So you have an appropriate plan of how long you are going to live, but because you are not in touch with the Soul you cannot see this plan. Sometimes, however, you can feel that it is time for you to go, and sometimes you can also feel when it is time for another person to go. You can actually feel that that person (maybe your husband, wife, child, or a friend or relative, or somebody you know) is going to die very soon, because you happen to tune into the person's Soul-Consciousness, even if that person might not be able to tune into it. Sometimes it is also possible to know in advance *how* they are going to die.

The causes of death are always karmic—not only in the sense of individual Karma, but planetary Karma. Humanity has a massive Karma, so there is a choice of ways to die: accidents, heart attacks, cancer, or many others. What is important is not the way you die but the fact that you have to die. It is compulsory for you to liberate yourself from this restricting, limiting condition and to move on to the next dimension; otherwise you become crystallized.

The Soul is joyful when you die, because finally you can breathe. When you return to the Astral World you have a much larger life, a much larger life-force. It is a liberating process and you feel a sense of freedom, happiness and joy. That is why nobody should be afraid of death because it is a return to a larger condition.

No Need to Fear Death

Because of materialistic consciousness many think that all there is to life is what they see, feel, hear and touch, so consequently people are often afraid of death. Unfortunately some religions have taught that this is your one and only life, and you either go 'down' or you go 'up' with no other alternative. This horrible doctrine has been forced on people since the fourth century. If you don't know that you existed before and that it is natural to exist afterward, if you don't know that life itself is eternal and that you are part of the eternal Life-Stream, then of course you are afraid of death.

Nowadays there is even technology to prolong the life of the physical body. As technology improves, more people will be on life support or in artificial arrangements that allow the physical body to survive. Why? Because the medical profession does not believe that life goes on. They believe that only *this* world exists, that when you die you forever cease to be, so naturally they want to save you, to extend this life a little longer, not realizing that *you always have been alive* and you always will be alive, with or without your body.

Another reason why many people are afraid of death is that they feel they will become disconnected from their friends or loved ones. You are not losing your loved ones when you die; on the contrary, you are connecting more strongly with them.

When you are out of your physical body, your total sense of awareness is within your astral body, which feels a thousand times more strongly than when the physical body was blocking it. On the other side you will be able to pick up everybody's feelings far more intensely than in normal life, so this is why it is important for people who are alive in the physical body to not generate negative emotions towards those who have died. The astral body is a tremendous sensory mechanism and the deceased become affected by the emotions of the living (unless they are very advanced and are able to deal with the impressions). If someone is depressed, they will feel it; if someone is happy, they will feel it. The fact to remember is that they are registering emotions more strongly than ever.

What Happens When You Die?

When you die you simply step out of your physical body and find yourself exactly as you were before. You are no different, because the physical body is not you. Your sense of "I", your feeling nature and your thinking process, have no relation to your physical body at all. When you step out of your body and enter the astral dimension, you still feel exactly as you felt before and you still think exactly as you thought before—you *are* exactly as you were before, without the slightest change. You might see your physical body as being strange and wonder, who on earth is that person? But as an entity you have not changed. It is important to understand this, because it is another false idea that when you die you somehow become different. You only become different by changing yourself *before* death, not afterwards.

What you *think* when you die or what you *feel* when you die gives you an indication of what you are going to be on the other dimensions, according to the Law of Attraction. If you die in a state of absolute anger, hate, violence or fear, then naturally you will go to the regions of the astral dimension that resonate with those vibrations. The Astral World is a vast world of vibrating energies and each energy has its own wavelength. Fear has its own wavelength; anger has its own wavelength; violence, hate and ignorance have their own wavelength. It is *how you feel and how you think* when you die that determines your fate.

The Astral World has seven subplanes, each of which vibrates to a certain frequency, and as an average or normal person (not an Adept, Master or Saint) you go to the region that suits your emotional condition. If you were habitually angry all of your life and the vibration of anger is strong in your astral body, then when you die you will go to a lower region of the Astral World where anger is a stable vibration. If you were joyful and happy, then you will go to an upper region of the Astral World where joy and happiness are the normal vibration. If you were an artist, for instance, and were always experiencing beautiful, inspired feelings and creative energies, then naturally you will experience the upper regions of the Astral World where the feelings are very refined.

In other words, nobody is going to *tell* you where to go. There is no Being or God on the other side who punishes you in any way, who says you were bad so you go down, or you were good so you go up. It is just the Law of Universal Nature at work. After death you are *automatically* attracted to the condition that matches your vibration.

That Law also works the same way in *this* world. You may notice that you are often attracted to people with whom you are able to sympathize. Your astral body and the other person's astral body are similar, so you are attracted to each other, even in this world. In the afterlife this is totally, one hundred percent the Law: whatever the state of your emotional body, you attract to yourself that particular vibration. And in the Inner Worlds there is every possible vibration, from the densest darkness to the most exalted feelings of joy and happiness—it is all there in graded vibration.

The Inner Worlds are Not New to Us

Suppose you have made this transition and you are in the Astral World. You may have been taught by the church that God created you for this lifetime only, and that upon death you go either to Heaven or to Hell. Not knowing anything about the afterlife, you presume that Heaven or Hell will be a new place for you. This is not the reality. You have already known the Astral World in which you find yourself.

The astral dimension is not new for us, and the mind dimension is not new for us—nothing is new for us in the Inner Worlds. We have been there for aeons and aeons already, so when you leave your physical body you suddenly find yourself in an environment that you already know. The only exceptions are those people who died while in a negative emotional state which had enough power to paralyse the function of the astral body.

The astral body is always moving and changing like a flowing stream. Certain intense emotions, such as violence, fear, depression or anger, can paralyse and block it, and then the astral body just circulates around within that blocked energy. There are people whose energies have become locked into a pattern by the sudden shock of being murdered, or dying a violent death in an accident, war, suicide or something similar. Instead of naturally experiencing the real possibilities and greatness of the Astral World, they get locked into the negative emotion that was generated before the moment of death and consequently that emotional mood is the only thing they experience, over and over. *That* is the real Hell because their consciousness is unable to perceive anything else around them. If the emotion was very intense, their attention becomes so involved in it that nobody can help them on the other side, even though somebody who is wide awake on the Astral Plane may be aware of their condition.

Those who are aware and able to function normally in the inner dimensions can see the problem, but they cannot help because those circulating in that emotional pattern are not open enough to register any external vibration. They have locked themselves into a cage. They can only be helped when that emotional force starts to weaken after some years, sometimes many years. Then they can slowly expand and become aware of the environment around them, the people, objects, colours and entities of the Astral World.

In accordance with the Law of the Inner Worlds, upon death your *feeling* will determine your destiny. At a later stage, when you rise above the Astral World into the Mental World, it is your *thinking* which will guide your destiny, and that can be lower thinking, higher thinking, or bright, sheer Intelligence.

The Second Death

You can live in the Astral World for a number of years—twenty years, a hundred or even many hundreds of years. It depends again on your emotional life. If you have no emotional life, no inner vibration of any kind, then you quickly come back into incarnation because the only thing you are attracted to is this physical life, the physical vibration of this world.

Suppose you are a feeling person and you lived a feeling life. After death you live in your astral body in the Astral World, feeling and thinking as the individual "you" until all of your feelings have been exhausted and it is time for you to die again. This is known as the *Second Death*. Your astral body stops functioning for a moment, just as your physical body stops functioning at physical death, and you simply step out of your astral body and find yourself in your mind-body, the thinking body. And you realize that you are still the real you! This second death in the Astral World corresponds to physical death although now the emphasis is on your *thoughts*.

The Mental World has seven subplanes, and according to your thinking-pattern you will be drawn to one or another of those subplanes. If your thoughts are of a very high vibration, you go to the higher regions of the Mental World. If your thoughts are of a low vibration, then you go to the lower regions. Whatever your thoughts, you find your own grade and automatically go there.

What determines how long you stay in the Mental World is the strength of your mental life while in the physical dimension. If you engaged your mind a lot—like metaphysicians and philosophers, for instance—you naturally will stay longer because the mental waves you generated may be enough to last for thousands of years. The greater your mental activity, the longer the time you spend in the Mental World.

The Third Death

This is all a natural progression. You have been to the Physical, Astral and Mental Worlds, and you have exhausted all the mental ideas that you could have about anything. Then comes the *Third Death*. You freeze for a moment in your mental body, step out of your mental body and find yourself as the Living Soul in your Radiant Body—the body that never dies and is never born—and you as a Living Soul realize yourself as the immortal and timeless Being you really are. You may do that for an instant or for a long period of time; it depends on how Soul-Conscious you were before you died. The length of all these time periods in the Inner Worlds depends on how much you were attuned to those corresponding vibrations during your physical life.

So you have gone through the whole cycle, have died three times and find yourself existing as a free living entity, a timeless Living Soul within the radiant causal body. It is here that you can perceive all of your past lives simultaneously. All of your many lives and experiences are there for you right at that moment. You know exactly what progress you have made, and you know also what progress you made in your last lifetime. Your whole Life-stream is summed up in a little flicker of energy floating around in your causal body. You know that each flicker of energy is a particular lifetime, and you know the essence and the learned lessons of each of those lifetimes, how your last lifetime related to the other lifetimes, and whether you made things better or worse for yourself.

While in this state of the *Freedom of the Soul*, the Soul might have an inner notion such as, "I must incarnate and finish a job that I started in Egypt three thousand years ago but didn't complete." Then, in that condition as a Living Soul, subtle changes take place and you know that you are about to enter into incarnation again, to start a new creative cycle and start your journey downwards into the lower regions of Creation. It is at this point, when the Soul decides to incarnate again, that the Soul is telepathically in touch with the Lords of Karma.

The Lords of Karma are angelic hierarchies and to them Karma just means forces and energy-vibrations. They tune into your Soul, to your energy-patterns, the results of your past lives over aeons of time, and they suggest to your Soul that you work along a particular energy-line. They find a solution, the next stage for you. This is rather miraculous because these Angels are of such a high order that the past, present and future exist simultaneously within their Beings. There is simply a telepathic communication between those Angels and your Soul, and the Soul understands that it is supposed to work in this particular type of vibration for the coming life. The Soul then receives a pattern, and it starts building and working with that energy-field which the Soul hopes will achieve what is needed.

And then the whole process starts again. Along come the Angelic Hierarchies who help to build you a new mental body, a new astral body and a new etheric-physical body according to the pattern laid out for them. Finally (hopefully) you find some parents who actually want to understand what you are doing! So the incarnation process happens again; you are born back into this world and cry, "Waaa!" (What am I doing here again?)

Life is a most miraculous thing. You should not be afraid of death because it is just part of your life. If once you understand that Life is a large, timeless moment, then you will look upon every day you live and everything you do in life as part of that larger picture. ✴

Love & Wisdom
THE MEANING OF LIFE

CHAPTER 6

"The power of Love is cosmic and universal in all of Creation, hence
it is reflected back upon us so that we also have this power of Love,
Wisdom and Understanding within us. If God is Love, then there is only
one real objective in existence for us, and that is to become Love."

The Moment of Judgment

If you can understand the following statement about the Being of Light and the moment of Judgment, then you have already sorted out your life's purpose and you are on the way to Enlightenment.

> At the Hour of Judgment, the Being of Light will ask only two questions of you: how much Love did you express towards all human beings you met in your life; and how much True Knowledge (Wisdom) did you gather while living in your physical body. Only these two things are important: Love and Wisdom.

We begin this life with certain qualities—and this has nothing to do with our genes! Modern science has the idea that the genetic code we inherit biologically from our parents determines everything. It doesn't. It determines the quality of the *physical* body—that is all. Our mental qualities are our own, our emotional qualities are our own and our Soul-qualities are our own. We do inherit physical attributes from our parents, but they are the least important. Our real Being includes that which we inherit from past lifetimes.

So we start this life with a pattern, which is a summary of all our past lives up until we entered the inner dimensions after our last incarnation. This summary reflects a specific rate of consciousness-vibration with which we are born in this life to start again. During this life we can modify this consciousness-vibration, and we always do, for better or worse. In other words, if you were a great Saint in your last lifetime, it doesn't automatically mean you will remain a Saint in this lifetime. Consciousness is fluidic; you can change it at will, moment by moment.

The important point is that when you die you will face the Being of Light within you. We all have to. It only takes a moment or two, and in that moment of Judgment your consciousness is pierced directly by the Being of Light, and you will see your entire past shown to you as a sequence of *transformations* of your consciousness. You will realize very clearly that the essence of all those transformations depends on two things: your ability to *love* and your ability to be *wise,* that is, to profoundly understand the mystery of life. Literally, nothing else matters.

This is a shocking revelation for people who are very busy, those who are world-shakers achieving name and fame for themselves in society. They think they are storing up good deeds in Heaven by accumulating a lot of money, prestige or success, but in the end it counts for nothing. At the moment of Judgment, no worldly achievement is asked of you.

An important point here is that once you realize what is emphasized in Divine Consciousness, you understand what it is you should emphasize in your life. You realize that the best thing to do in life is to develop the capacity for Wisdom and the capacity to truly love, for this is the real purpose of life—not all those other things that people say you should be striving for as the meaning of life. Earning money so you can feed, house and clothe your body is a physical necessity, nothing more and nothing less. You naturally and spontaneously fulfil your duties toward your family, your job, your nation and Humanity, but you know your life's real direction and that is where you are focused. This does not mean that you give up life and become a renunciate; that would be a wrong interpretation. Rather, your true aim is to understand where your Heart and Soul should be directed. Jesus said, "Seek ye first the Kingdom of God and all other things will be added unto you" (Matthew 6: 33).

The goals of Humanity are completely in the wrong direction, and when you encounter the Being of Light you will see which of your actions were completely in the wrong direction. This is not a philosophy;

it makes absolutely no difference whether you believe it or not. This is what is going to happen to you at the end of your life journey.

The Seven Cosmic Attributes

If you are a logical person, you may ask why it is that you struggle all your life to achieve all manner of things but in the end you are asked to account for only two qualities: Love and Wisdom. Nothing else. Why not other qualities? Why not your success in business or art or any other area? There is a profound reason why this is so, and it has to do with the Cosmos itself, with the Divine Intelligence as it manifests through us.

The Divine Intelligence manifests simultaneously on all levels of the Cosmos according to seven great types of activity, or attributes, of Divinity—the Godhead within all Creation. I will enumerate for you these seven great archetypal energies of Divinity; then I will explain how these are reflected in the Solar System and in human consciousness, so that you understand why the Love aspect is so important for this particular planetary civilization.

The first of these great attributes of Divinity is *Will* and *Power*. Throughout every part of Creation, the Divine Intelligence always works according to Plan, Purpose and Will, and of course it has the infinite Power to do so. It does not work in a haphazard, hit-and-miss way. If you could travel interdimensionally through Space, you would soon notice that this quality of Divinity—planning, purpose, incredible Power and Will—is everywhere. You may call it the quality of rulership or kingship throughout all of Creation. And here is an important point: because you are *part* of Divinity, you also have some of that quality of Power, Will, Purpose, Plan and Divine Kingship developed to a certain degree within *you*. In human terms it expresses itself through leadership—as in kings, emperors, presidents and leaders.

The second great attribute of Divinity is that of *Love, Wisdom* and *Understanding*, the compassionate understanding of all creatures, all behaviour patterns, all growth processes, and so on. The power of Love is cosmic and universal in all of Creation, hence it is reflected back upon us so that we also have this power of Love, Wisdom and Understanding within *us* (to whatever degree it has developed). It can manifest in human society as the ability to heal, for instance. So there is that first great Power that knows the Plan and enforces the Plan by Will, simultaneously working with this second attribute which understands through Love, Wisdom and Compassion.

The third great attribute of Divinity is *Intelligence, Activity* and *Organization*. The Divine Creator (the Absolute) has the quality of ceaseless Activity, and the power to intelligently organize Creation, in the form of little things like galaxies and universes! The universe is incredibly vast but nevertheless it is all subject to *intelligent activity*. This intelligent activity and organizing ability is part of the Divine Mind, an attribute of Divinity, and according to the level of our development it is also reflected within us.

The fourth great cosmic attribute is that of *Harmony* and *Beauty*. If you could see the whole mechanism of Creation with total vision, from both inside and outside, you would notice that it is patterned according to laws of Beauty and Harmony. Those divine qualities are reflected in human nature and are expressed through the fields of mathematics, geometry, music and all forms of art. Because the entire Universe is in harmony, it expresses beauty—and once again that is reflected in us so that we also manifest those qualities.

The fifth great cosmic attribute is *Reason, Logic* and *Objectivity*. The reasoning faculty of the Divine Mind creates what we call the "objective view". In that moment of being seen objectively, the object—such as a planet, a solar system, a galaxy, a human being or an angel—becomes objectified (created). Everything in Creation has been objectified in the Divine Mind. This Divine Reason is another part of the tremendous Cosmic Intelligence that brings everything into expression, into objective form. Of course, we have that ability too; in human consciousness it is mainly expressed through the scientific way of thinking.

The sixth cosmic attribute is that of *Divine Worship,* or the creation of *the ideal Archetype.* In Humanity it can express itself as worship of the Deity or as the fanatical attempt to become some ideal. It may be the ideal of the Christ, the Buddha, Kṛṣṇa, or Rāma, or it may be a political or religious ideal where you have some idea in your mind and pour your whole life-stream into it. Many of the early philosophers were idealists. Most systems of government are created by idealistic people who have an idea they develop into an ideal, and then other people work with that ideal as if it was the ultimate reality. So there is this quality in the Divine Mind that creates the ideal Archetype, towards which the whole of Creation is moving in its growth and unfoldment, and by reflection it enters human consciousness as the *worship* of an ideal, or as devotion towards something or someone.

The seventh great quality of Divinity is that of *Law* and *Order.* The great Cosmic Mind, Divinity, sets up a way of doing things in the Cosmos: how a planet or solar system should function, what the relationship between two galaxies should be, or how the invisible universe should relate to something else. In other words, in the Divine Consciousness, there is a certain way of doing things, and this is reflected back into us as the human quality of orderliness, or a ritualistic, systematic way of doing things.

So, in summary, you now know that the Universe—the *total* Universe, in all its visible and invisible manifestation—is guided by these seven great qualities or universal laws. And, because we are part of Divinity, by reflection these Laws are also functioning within us.

In the Divine Reality, these seven qualities are functioning simultaneously, in a unified state, permeating every layer of Reality. Within the great cosmic picture, however, this Universal Manifestation can be broken down further into smaller units. For instance, in some galaxies the second quality (the quality of Love) is the chief or dominating power. In another galaxy it may be the quality of Harmony. In another it may be the quality of orderly Activity or Will-Power. Although there is one Universal Manifestation, different aspects of Creation emphasize a certain quality above the others, into which the other qualities merge.

At this point you might like to pause and look at yourself, and consider how many of those divine qualities you have developed within you. You may have a lot of those qualities or you may have only a few. During aeons of incarnating you may have developed certain qualities and completely neglected some of the others. This can provide an insight into your nature on the personality level. What are your strengths and weaknesses? What is your forte?

Our Solar System and Love

So we are coming down from the universal scale to the galactic scale, and now to *our Solar System,* which by comparison is on a very small scale. When interdimensional space is considered, however, our Solar System is a much larger structure than we realize. With physical vision all that can be seen are the physical planets circulating around a glowing ball of hydrogen, but the actual reality is not like that at all.

Our Solar System actually contains seventy-two planets. The known planets are just those planets that have physical bodies, while the remainder are invisible planets on the Etheric, Astral, Mental, Buddhic and Nirvāṇic Planes. (Refer to Endnote, page 244.) The Solar System exists on seven great planes or dimensions, intertwining and whirling like clockwork, wheels within wheels, and within that inner space the seventy-two planets are functioning in a network of energies. It is a complex and wonderful organism, a living body, a living Intelligence, a far more awesome vision than how it appears on the physical level.

Within the galaxy itself, the Seven Cosmic Attributes are divided between the millions of Solar Logoi, and each Solar Logos (Sun) specializes and focuses on one attribute (even though, remember, these attributes are simultaneously functioning everywhere).

Our Solar Logos is an average Solar Logos in this part of the Cosmos. He is that great Divine Being who inhabits this part of space and in whom "we live and move and have our being"—quite literally. Of those Seven Rays (Divine Attributes) *He expresses the quality of Divine Love, Wisdom and Compassion as the goal of His evolution.* Eternity after eternity, aeon after aeon, He works along that line until He fully establishes that divine quality of Love and Wisdom. Another Solar Logos may express one of the other qualities, but for the time being we are just talking about our particular Sun.

The other qualities still exist within the consciousness of our Solar Logos, and therefore within our solar-systemic organization, nevertheless, the chief quality expressed by our Solar Logos is the power of Love, attraction, cohesion or healing, and the power of Understanding or Wisdom. Because the Love and Wisdom aspect is the main quality expressed by our Solar Logos, *everything in our Solar System must tend towards that quality, and in the end become that quality.* This gives you the clue as to why Love and Wisdom are so important for us.

God is Love and We Must Become Love

Now let us come down further in scale to the *Human Monad*. The Monad is the Divine Spirit, a little flame of the Cosmic Fire of the Sun embedded in you. It is the *Being of Light*, that ultimate Ruling Principle of your Soul over an eternity of lifetimes.

Now, here we are coming to the understanding of your true human significance: because the Human Monad is a reflection of our Solar Logos, whose main quality is Love and Wisdom, then naturally the Monad within us is made purely out of this quality. It also has the other qualities, of course, but Love and Wisdom predominate. This means that over aeons of time, the whole human evolutionary process on this planet is subjected to the law of Love and the law of Wisdom. The Monad within us teaches the Soul that this is the only lesson of existence, the only reason to be; and by reflection, the Soul tries to teach the personality, incarnation after incarnation, that the only meaning of life is Love and Wisdom, with the other qualities being only accessories.

This truth summarizes your whole life: *God is Love and we must become Love.* The goal is always Love because God is Love. God *here* is the Solar Logos, the great Cosmic Being in our part of space in whom all the planets live, and in whom we and all the Creative Hierarchies live. There are twelve Creative Hierarchies simultaneously evolving in our Solar System—the Human Hierarchy, the Angelic Hierarchy, the Archangelic Hierarchy, and so on—and they all must tend towards Love, no matter what other attributes they may have or express. The ultimate goal is to merge all those other attributes into the power of Love and Wisdom, which is the very essence of our God-Being, our Solar Logos.

This is the truth of how Nature functions in this part of Creation: by the power of Love. Because the Solar Logos is Love, all the individual Monads in the Solar System are based on Love, therefore the individual Souls (which are based on the Monads) are based on Love, and therefore we must base our individual *personalities* on the Soul-pattern, which is Love.

I am trying to tell you a very important point. Hopefully this will explain to you why, when you die, you are not going to be examined on your artistic attributes, your logical-mind attributes, your willpower or whatever. This is a spiritual principle, not a philosophy invented by the human mind. I am talking about knowledge that comes from a deeper consciousness, which you can find out for yourself only when you reach that deeper consciousness. Once you reach Cosmic Consciousness, and beyond to the sixth level of consciousness or above, then you will realize exactly what I am saying.

So this is what you are supposed to be learning from the time you are put on this planet as a human being. However, the existential problem is that in the beginning we do not know this. For many lifetimes the Soul is trying to impress onto the personality this quality of Love and Wisdom, but the personality doesn't comprehend it, or is not able to put it into practice. So we express ourselves and develop all kinds of wonderful qualities over many lifetimes, but most of the time we neglect the most important one, the quality of Love. You may become the greatest scientist, the greatest artist, the greatest leader; you may have all these other wonderful powers and qualities but completely neglect the field of Love. Consequently, people have to be pushed into incarnation again and again until the Soul manages to convince the personality that the only meaning of any lifetime relates to that sublime question at the moment of death: Did you love? Did you attain Wisdom? If the answer is no, then back into the reincarnation cycle you go until finally you wake up and do the right thing during your life.

Our Way of Return is Love

Because we now know how wonderfully and profoundly the Cosmos is designed, we should be wise and start working along this line: if God is Love, then there is only one real objective in existence for us, and that is *to become Love*. If we can become Love, then we can be released and reabsorbed—firstly back into the Soul-Nature, then from the Soul-Nature back into the Monad (the Divine Spirit within us), then from the Divine Spirit back into the Solar-Logoic Essence, the very Heart of Divine Love in our Universal Manifestation. We then have achieved the Goal for which we were projected into existence. We came into manifestation through the power of Love, and by the power of Love we can return.

Each Human Monad is projected out of the Solar Fire. Within the Sun, in interdimensional space, there is a huge blaze of Fire—not physical fire but spiritual Fire, a white heat out of which the Monads are thrown off into interdimensional space like little sparks. The Monads themselves then throw off the Living Soul, and the Living Soul throws itself off into the personality. There is an ever-descending order of reality—but we have to *reverse* it. So the personality has to become the Living Soul by the power of Love; the Living Soul has to become the Monad by the power of Love; the Monad has to become the Solar Logos (our Deity) by the power of Love. The way back is Love! In this Solar System, the rule of Love is the absolute Law to which everything must conform at the end of time.

So this is an important understanding for you. You should reflect on that very profound statement about the moment of Judgment, otherwise you will again "miss the boat" in this lifetime, or in the future, until you realize that no matter what else you have achieved, if you didn't follow the Law of Love you will be cast back into incarnation again and again.

You may have developed certain qualities, and that is good. Those are universal, divine qualities of Beingness that we all have to varying degrees, but we must also understand that although we may have all these wonderful qualities—whether in art, intelligent activity, logic, reason or the ability to plan—we must subjugate them to the law of Love.

You might say, very disgustedly, that you are a great artist who has created great works of art. Or you may be a great scientist, with a wonderfully logical mind, who has created many inventions. You may have become a great politician and led a great nation—and that is fine too. Unfortunately, the spiritual fact of life is that you will not be tested on those accomplishments.

If you have all these other wonderful qualities, you must use them totally and absolutely for the service of all Life. That is your gift. Any great quality you have is a divine quality, and through those divine qualities you serve Creation; that is your means of service, the means through which you express your Love. If you are an artist, you pour your Love-energy into your art. If you are a scientist, your science is your field of service. If you are a leader, then it is through your leadership that you serve. But if there is no Heart in it, forget it; in evolutionary terms it means nothing.

Remember, this is not prejudice against those other qualities; it is simply an existential Law of the Solar System that cannot be changed. If you happen to be in another Solar System where some other quality is the predominant quality, then the priority would be to develop that quality. But it so happens that you are here now and you cannot alter that fact; you just have to follow the rule, and the rule for us is the Law of Love and Wisdom. All the Creative Hierarchies in this Solar System have to learn this as the main evolutionary qualification.

So don't be discouraged; those other qualities are there to be used, but if they are not expressed through the quality of Love or through the quality of Wisdom, then you have still missed your destiny as a human being on this planet. If you have not developed the qualities of Love and Wisdom, then the Being of Light will make sure you have another opportunity to practise those two qualities—maybe a thousand more lifetimes! The opportunity will be provided until you learn the qualities of Love and Wisdom. All that will be asked of you at the most crucial moment of your life—the moment of death—is how much Love and Wisdom you have gained. You may make a list of all the other good things you have done and it won't even be noticed. But did you love somebody? You will be reminded of even your smallest deed of Love.

What Is Love and Wisdom?

Now we have to talk about what Love really is, because Love is the whole meaning of human existence. Many people think that if they give twenty dollars to some charity or another, then they are showing a powerful Love. But that is not Love; it is something else. Merely giving money to charity is very useful and helpful for that charity, but it does not show any Love inside you whatsoever.

I am trying to tell you that Love is a quality of the Heart. It doesn't matter whether you are rich or poor; your ability to give is not dependent on your wealth. Very often, poor people think, "Oh, I cannot help people because I have no money!" But in fact, money has no relevance to helpfulness at all. You can be the poorest person, possessing absolutely nothing, but if your Heart is expanded towards another person—a person who is suffering or who requires your attention—and your Heart is totally in it, then *that* is Love. Even if you didn't give a single cent, the reward is instantaneous, the divine transformation has occurred. Your loving action is noticed and registered instantaneously by the Being of Light within you.

Furthermore, sometimes people pretend to love. For instance, maybe a parent pretends to love his child by sending the child to an expensive school but with no real inner feeling for the child whatsoever. Of course, people think, "What a loving parent—look at all those expensive schools and toys." But that is not loving. In fact, there is no Love in it whatsoever. It is just convenience. Love is much more than what most people think it is.

Jesus tried to explain the Path of Love. Jesus was attuned to His own Monad (He called the Monad within Him, "the Heavenly Father"), and He knew that the Law was nothing else but Love and Wisdom. He was trying to illustrate the difference between real Love and charity, and the example He used was the rich man in the synagogue who was supposed to be demonstrating Love. This rich man arrogantly threw shekels here and there, with trumpets blasting, and so on. Jesus was watching the scene and said to the Disciples, "That guy won't get to Heaven, that is for sure." What the rich man was doing was for show; he was arrogant and proud and there was no Love in his action whatsoever. He could have given all his wealth, but without Love it still would have meant nothing. Then Jesus told the Disciples to observe an old woman, sitting unnoticed in an unimportant place in the same synagogue. She had only a few shekels, which were probably a month's savings from her tea-money, or something like that, and she quietly dropped her few shekels into the box. Jesus said, "She is the one who will go to Heaven." (Mark 12: 38-44)

Love is an attitude of Inner Consciousness; it is not what you give outwardly. Love is the way you *are*. It is what comes *out* of you, what actually dwells in your Heart in any given circumstance. This is where you will be tested by the Being of Light when you die. It is your Heart that is tested; not your outer action, but what is *behind* the outer action.

Jesus was trying to teach his pupils examples from real life. He also told the story about a person travelling to another town who was robbed and beaten to the ground. Along came a rich person on his donkey who, as did many others, looked at the mugged person and just carried on. Then came along a very poor person with a good Heart, and he picked the man up, took him home and fed him. And Jesus said, "*That* is Love".

Jesus also gave the example of a man in prison whose friend came to visit him. In this parable, notice that Jesus didn't say that this guy was in prison and the friend came along and gave him one thousand shekels and therefore everyone was happy! No, Jesus just said, "He came and visited him." The act of visiting, consoling and nourishing him was the loving deed—not bringing money or anything else. It was the Heart-to-Heart connection. Again, Jesus was trying to illustrate the fact that Love is an attitude of the Heart. It is the way you are towards human beings, towards animals, towards all of Creation, towards God. It has nothing to do with wealth or prestige, power or position, name or fame. It is the simple acts you do through the power of Love that are registered in Eternity. It is how you are. What we have to learn in this lifetime is to just be ourselves in Lovingness.

This Love is the same as true healing energy. For instance, you may go to a doctor who works only for money, and because he has no loving Heart he prescribes you something and you go away and feel nothing. Another time you may visit a doctor who is truly concerned about you—that is, his Heart Chakra is awake and sending out loving vibrations—and you come away from that doctor feeling really good! This is another example that Love is the Heart energy-vibration that you give out to others. At the moment of death, your destiny is immediately determined by the growth of Love within your Heart.

Saint Paul was also trying to teach this Love, which he learned directly from Jesus. He said, "If I have this power or that power, if I can speak like the angels, if I have all these things but have not Love, I am nothing." (1 Corinthians: 13) He was trying to say that people have different virtues, powers or abilities—what they called *the seven gifts of the Holy Spirit* (we call them the seven great Cosmic Attributes, Rays or Divine Powers). He was teaching the new Christians that Love is the only power on which you will be judged by the Being of Light.

So I encourage you to express the power of Love in your life. It means that you turn your Heart towards the sufferer, whether it is your friend in hospital, a person in prison, a suffering animal or people suffering in another country. Whenever you are aware of suffering, let your Heart go out to it and a magical transformation will take place. In that moment you are in the presence of the Being of Light, and that moment is registered as if it was a solid object; it is never forgotten for all Eternity. And strangely enough, many of your other successful achievements will not even be registered.

You may be a sportsman who has trained for twenty years, and finally you manage to get to the top. You get your gold medal, everybody praises you, and when you meet the Being of Light after death it is not even considered—as if it never happened! But suppose, after achieving this great name and fame, you saw an injured dog, and you picked up this suffering dog and took it home. You nursed him, bandaged him, showed some Love towards him. That was registered! All that vast effort you put towards achieving worldly success is not even counted, but that little deed of helping the dog is immediately shining, clear and bright, in cosmic memory.

Love can be expressed through us with infinite variety and possibilities; it can be expressed through the most trivial thing. For instance, if there is a little bug on the ground, some people just squash it. But, if you are a loving person, you take the bug and put it aside so that nobody will walk on it. That action is registered because it shows that your Heart was sympathetic towards the existence of that little bug. That apparently trivial deed is actually important and is registered. So Love doesn't require a huge charity ball. Real Love is these little things you do in life for others, for your family and friends, for the world at large, for anybody or anything you meet, whether it is a plant, a tree, an animal, a human being, an angel or God.

And what of Wisdom? Wisdom is the degree to which you respond correctly to the flow of events throughout your life. It is very different to the intellectual learning of worldly education—there is no textbook on it. Many people think they have acquired the quality of Wisdom because they have learned mathematics or nuclear physics at school or university. But that is not Wisdom! It is just learning. At the moment of death, intellectual knowledge is not even looked at; rather, the depths of your inner consciousness are probed.

Wisdom is how your inner consciousness views life, how it registers the whole life process—both your internal changes and the relationship of your consciousness to everything outside yourself. It is something that has arisen between your Soul-connection and you as a personality through your loving acts in life.

The Meaning of Divine Forgiveness

There was once a highway robber who, with his band of robbers, used to rob and kill people. One day, however, he had a flash of insight, that is, for one moment his Soul managed to communicate something to his personality, and at that moment something changed inside him. The Heart-connection was made between the Soul and the personality. He began to seek the Path and approach Teachers, and finally he became one of the great saints of India. His life completely changed: from being a vicious person he became an extraordinarily loving being.

I am saying that whatever you have been in your past—whether or not you have been a "sinner"—is not the important point. What is important is that moment when you awaken to the principle of Love and begin to apply it. At that moment you are a new person and a new life begins inside you. You might have been the most horrible murderer in your lifetime, but if suddenly you connect to your Heart and Soul, a radical transformation takes place and from that moment on you are living in the Light of Love. The Law of Love is yours! In that moment you gain a new understanding and, strange as it may seem, when you go to the other side, all your sins, viciousness, or whatever, will not even be considered. What will be counted is how you expressed that Love and Wisdom, from that moment onwards in your life.

So that is the good news. And if you truly understand this, it can radically change your life, just as it changed the lives of so many saints, whether Sufi, Jewish, Christian, Muslim, Buddhist or Hindu. At a certain moment they became new people and they were judged by the Divine Being inside them according to that new pattern, the Law of Love, rather than on anything that took place before that moment. That is the real meaning of Divine Forgiveness, or Divine Grace.

So this is the great encouragement from that wonderful statement we started with about the Being of Light: to remember where you are heading in your life. All of us are heading towards that moment when we have to face the Being of Light inside us, and we have to answer that question about our lives. It is not so much about what we did wrong, but what we did right. In other words, in which situation did we act with the power of Love? In which situation did we exercise our Heart?

If you understand the need for Love, the power of Love, and if you manage to live by it from this moment on, then you might say, "Hey, one day I have to face the Being of Light! It may be tonight, it may be tomorrow, it may be the day after. Am I ready for it? What am I going to say?" In actual fact, you won't need to say anything. You won't even be asked; the result will just be there. You will simply know how it is. And, unfortunately, there are no appeals. If you come to that very critical moment and find not a single instant in your life when you truly acted out of Love, then that is very bad news. You may list any other qualities you want, but they will not even be considered. You simply return to the cycle of reincarnation.

So it is very heartening to know that in order to attain this wonderful state of Divine Consciousness and move upward in spiritual evolution, we don't have to do much. Isn't it wonderful that we don't have to do much? All we have to do is be loving! Wherever and however we are, *be loving!* So there is hope for all of us, because the Way of Love can be practised by every single human being on this planet, in any situation. Love can be expressed through us with infinite variety and possibilities—the opportunity is literally everywhere. What demonstrates the growth of your Soul, the understanding of your Soul and the understanding between your personality and your Soul, is the Love and Wisdom that you express through your Heart. It is what matters now and in the future. In the end it is the only thing that matters. ⚹

Karma
HOW TO BREAK FREE OF ITS CHAINS

CHAPTER 7

"With this understanding you realize the awesome responsibility
of being in incarnation, because everything—whether you
think it, feel it or do it—has an impact on everything else."

*K*arma is a Sanskrit word which means "action" or "activity and its results". About one hundred years ago Western science discovered the idea that for every action there is an opposite reaction. The Ancients, however, already knew this for thousands of years, and it was taught openly in India, Greece, China and elsewhere. Science limits this idea to the action of matter and energy in this physical universe, whereas the Ancients understood that Karma works not only in this *physical* dimension but also on the *inner* dimensions: in the Astral World, the Mental World, the Causal World, and so on. Karma applies universally, whether we are talking about the Cosmos at large, the Solar System, a planet, human beings, angels, animals, or a single individual within a species.

Many people don't know about Karma, or if they do they have a very superficial knowledge: that it is just part of Hindu philosophy, for example, and does not relate to them personally. Karma is not just an idea or a philosophy; it is a very dynamic reality. You are here because of your karma, and your karma is guiding you every moment of your life. That is how real it is.

In this lifetime, everything you think leaves a trace on the mental structure of our planet; everything you feel leaves a wavelet of energy on the astral dimension of our planet; every action you perform leaves its own imprint on the etheric substance of the physical planet of our Earth. In other words, all your thoughts in your mental body, in the Mental World; all your feelings in your astral body, in the Astral World; all your actions in the physical body, in this Physical World, produce an *effect* or *karma*. Everything leaves an imprint, without exception.

The Ancients also realized that Karma is not only the repercussions from thoughts, feelings and actions in the *present* moment, it also involves the repercussions from thoughts, feelings and actions in the *past*. This is where you need the understanding of another topic: *Reincarnation*. Without an understanding of Reincarnation, the idea of past Karma does not make any sense.

So, as a fundamental principle of life, *everything we think, feel and do* has a repercussion, which needs another action to make it better or worse, and this activity just continues in cycles. With this understanding you realize the awesome responsibility of being in incarnation, because everything—whether you think it, feel it or do it—has an impact on everything else. The problem is that people have been incarnating for aeons and using Karma unintelligently. To use an analogy, it is like playing with electricity: every time you put your wet finger in a plug socket you get burnt, and you keep doing it because you have no idea that electricity does that.

Before we can understand Karma—how it is enslaving us at the moment, and how it can liberate us—we have to understand the vastness of Life: who we are, where we come from and where we are going. Then, in that big scheme of things, Karma makes perfect sense and we can start to use it intelligently.

The Vastness of Life

In the large cosmic scheme of things we start at the middle point: as *Living Souls* (Human Souls) in the Causal World. Each of us is an immortal Soul encased in a causal body. The causal body is also called the *Shining Body* because it is luminous and far more beautiful than the personality being—and it is eternal. Your mental body, your astral body and your etheric-physical body all disappear after each incarnation, but the causal body remains. So, this Living Soul, for experience or whatever reason, has decided to incarnate into the lower dimensions: the Mental World, the Astral World and the Physical World.

When the decision was made to descend from the harmonious Causal World, we were not told that there was going to be an invincible law that had to be obeyed—the Law of Karma—and that we would also incur karma in the process. The idea of descending into the Astral and Physical Worlds and having an exciting time there may have impressed the Soul, but if before descending we had fully comprehended the massive amount of karma that would need to be worked out, with all the suffering and the resulting problems, we would never have wanted to do it! If we *were* informed, then we didn't register it, or it simply wasn't understood. So, since ancient times we have been incarnating under the delusion that we are incarnating for experience.

Now you would think that after incarnating for one thousand lifetimes you would surely know the system and what the point of it all is, right? Yet people still do *not* know, they have absolutely no idea, and that is precisely the point. Therein lies the tragedy of Karma.

The Law of Karma is a very strict and unbending law with no exceptions. If you think you are an exception, beware! Even if you are the Prime Minister of China or the President of the United States, there is no exception; the Law is absolute. It is the Will of God, how God has ordained things to be, and the Divine Mind does not change. The beauty of the unchangeable Will of God, however, is that once you learn how Karma works then you can work with it *intelligently*, rather than opposing it all the time.

The Three Types of Karma

To work with Karma more intelligently it is important to understand that there are three types of Karma. The first type of Karma is what in Sanskrit is called SANCITTA KARMA, or what we call the *stored-up* Karma. It is stored as little energy-points of light and colour, shining and radiant, in your causal body. Strange as it may seem, in the Divine Will, each of these little energy-points is a record of your life. It's almost as if God created the microchip long before science did! Each energy-point is like a microchip containing the karmic record of a particular life in minute detail—all your actions, thoughts and feelings during that life—and your Causal (Soul) Intelligence can see it.

So even before you are born you have this massive record of stored-up Karma in your causal body, whether you are aware of it or not. It is the vast karma of the past, accumulated since the beginning of your evolution in Lemuria, Atlantis, and so on, and it just stays there, suspended in the 'computer' of your causal body, ready to spring into action when you 'open the file'. It is the primary source of the total destiny possible to you on this planet, from the beginning of time until the end of the evolutionary process. This understanding is very practical because it will help you know what to do in this lifetime in order to liberate yourself.

The second type of Karma is called PRĀRABDHA KARMA, or the *Karma to be worked out in this lifetime.* Before you are born, your Soul in the Heaven Worlds has a vision of the karma to be worked out in *this* lifetime. How do you decide which karmas you want to work out in this life? While in your own divinity as an immortal Soul, you scan the karmic energy-points in your causal aura and assess what needs to be worked out. You might say, "I harmed that person four lifetimes ago so I'd better do something about that" or "I married that person fifteen times and I still can't get along with her." So you have a plan of what karma you will work out in this lifetime, but it is still only a minute fragment of the total amount of karma stored in your causal body. Nevertheless, it is the karma that *you* decide you will attempt to amend in *this* particular lifetime, and you decide while you still have the inner vision and understanding of a Living Soul.

So then you start the whole process of incarnation again. You descend from the Heaven World into the Astral World then the Etheric-Physical World and finally you incarnate in a physical body as a baby. Every person is born with a very definite plan for this lifetime—all the things he or she needs to learn and to work out—but it is all forgotten. Why? Because the person's new physical body has no connection with its Causal Self, nor do its new astral body and new mental body, so there is no imprint from the causal body and the person is born without any clue of what the Soul's plan is! Life begins and then the winds of chance take over. (Among the billions of people, of course, there are those who manage to recover, or bring through, the plan that they had before incarnation, and therefore they can start working on it actively and intelligently. But they are the exceptions.)

The third type of Karma is called KRIYAMĀNA KARMA, or the *Karma we incur in this lifetime*. From the time you are born until the time you die, you think, feel and act, thus generating more karma. So you have this massive amount of karma stored-up in the background; the little bit that you are meant to work out in this lifetime, but have forgotten about; and on top of that you are generating more new karma in *this* lifetime.

This is why you need to start understanding how the fundamental laws of life work. Very few religions understand the total nature of how the Cosmos works, how the Divine Will works, and how we should relate intelligently to Divinity and to the Supernatural Law of the Cosmos. Karma is the Supernatural Law of the Cosmos—on the physical level and on all dimensions, in every aspect of, and beyond, Time and Space. If you don't understand it you are a lost soul, wherever you are.

Family Karma, National Karma and World Karma

In addition to the three main types of Karma that I have described above, let us now look at how Karma operates on the individual level and on the level of relationships such as families, nations, religions and humanity as a whole.

Some groups of Souls can have *family karma* if they have been incarnating within the same family structure many times, maybe as a husband, wife, child, brother, sister, uncle, and so on. Believe it or not, karma is interlinked in the Inner Worlds. If you are plugged into another family member's karma, and that person is connected to your karma, then there is an interaction between those karmas that makes things rather complicated. So it's not enough that you have to deal with your own baggage; you have to deal with everybody else's as well because you are part of that family's karma.

When you are on the Spiritual Path you have to consider your family karma. It can often be difficult for the average seeker to escape from his or her family because of the strong bond of family karma. As long as you behave the way the family wants you to, things are okay; if you don't you become a black sheep, cast out of the family grace. By nature, the family wants to hold you in bondage to what it has done for generations. So you may have to clash with your family, and you have to understand that.

Sometimes it may be difficult to do your spiritual work because your family, or some member of the family, may oppose it. This is part of your family karma so you have to take it into consideration and learn to work with it wisely. You have a choice. What will it be? Your Liberation? Or is it better to hold on to some family tradition and only do what the family says you should do? It is important that you analyse your life, otherwise you can be holding back your spiritual progress. Be kind to your family but at the same time be strong. Every type of karma, whether it is personal or family, is like a chain around your neck—a chain you need to break.

If that is not enough, *tribal karma* can be another chain around your neck. A clan or a tribe is actually the same thing as a family but it may involve several thousand people. They also put a huge pressure on you to conform, making it difficult for you to break out and enter the spiritual way of life.

You also have the karma of your *race*. Racial karma—whether your skin is white, black, yellow or any other colour—is just as real as your personal karma, and it can hold you back. There is also the karma of your *nation,* how you are supposed to act if you live in a particular country, and the karma of your *religion,* which says you have to behave in a certain way because you are a Christian, a Jew or a Muslim. Your country, your race and your religion are strong karmas which are acting upon you all the time.

Education is another karma imposed on people, particularly children. Education, under a religious or political dictatorship, communism or so-called democracies, can be a form of brainwashing. For instance, I was born in a communist country under the regime of Stalin, and at school we had to learn by heart all kinds of slogans: that in communism there is paradise and in communism the human being is the most important thing, and so on. Even completely nonpolitical subjects like Latin, science or ancient history were used as opportunities for brainwashing. Education is a leaning towards that which the authorities think is important, and it is another karma you have to deal with.

There are also the karmas *between* nations, the karmas *between* religions, and the karmas *between* races or tribes. These are complicated karmas which impact on hundreds of millions of people, and often lead to religious and political wars. This represents a huge amount of ongoing karma being worked out by millions and millions of people. Furthermore, these larger groupings also have their past stored-up karmas, the karmas being worked out in this lifetime and the karmas which are being generated now. When past karmas are precipitated in the present they can create a new set of karmas that will recur in the future. As an example, the wars between the Muslims and Christians during the times of the Crusades were precipitated from past stored-up karmas, which will be released again and will need to be worked out because they have not yet been resolved. Endless wars between nations or groups of people continue because they do not intelligently understand how to work out Karma: to connect to the Soul and understand the Plan behind it all.

There is also a large planetary karma, or *world karma*, which imposes a boundary on Humanity itself, limiting how far we can go, what we can do on the planet at this stage of human evolution. It is the boundary within which all the Human Souls (both in and out of incarnation) are bound by the Law of Karma.

Another consideration is the karma of special people like Saints and Yogīs. If you read about the lives of Indian Yogīs or Sufi, Jewish or Christian Saints, you find that, although they always fulfilled the Law and led a perfect and ideal lifestyle, they often suffered physically, emotionally or mentally without any apparent cause. You might ask, "How can that be? How can a holy person suffer so much?"

There was a great saint in India who died of a heart attack at a reasonably young age. There was seemingly no reason for him to die like that—he was a pure vegetarian, had no stress in his life and never acted or thought selfishly—but it was his Soul's choice to die at that time as part of his karma. Another example is Krishnamurti. He was a

Zen master with Buddhic and Nirvāṇic Consciousness, yet he suffered for forty years of his life with unbearable headaches and spinal pain. He didn't do anything about it; he never took painkillers or went to a doctor. Why? Because his Soul chose to work out a lot of karma so that he could liberate himself in his lifetime. Many people suffer much in life and, whether they are aware of it (as those Saints were) or not, it is their Soul's decision to pay back karma so that the Soul can be released for the greater Life and the greater Internal Reality.

So, it is important to have an understanding of all these types of Karma before you can enter the Path of Liberation. All our karmas are heavy chains holding us down, so is it any wonder that in any given age so few people attain Enlightenment?

The Spiritual Path and Karma

When you enter the Spiritual Path it becomes even more important to understand Karma, and to work with it intelligently and scientifically. Whether you succeed or flounder in your spiritual goal in this lifetime has to do with your karma and nothing else. It's as simple as that. This is why ninety-nine percent of students on the Spiritual Path never attain Enlightenment. Krishna said: "Out of every thousand people, one will seek me (that is, seek God, or seek Reality). And for every thousand that *seek* me, one will *find* me." So the proportion of those who attain is one one-thousandth multiplied by one one-thousandth—which is very small indeed! This is largely due to a lack of understanding of Karma and a lack of understanding of Life.

You have to understand the vastness of Karma before you can say, "Now I'm ready to go on the Spiritual Path. Now I understand what I have to do." You are the result of your individual karma and that of your family, race, religion, education, etc. Look at your life and see all ie factors that make you who you are, and then realize that they are all circumstantial and you don't have to be like that. Your limitations are not an absolute must but simply the circumstances that made you the way you are now. Realizing this is the first step on the great journey toward Liberation. Everybody has their own circumstantial karma—*everybody*—otherwise they would not be here. It is not a judgment on you or others; it is simply a recognition of the way things are.

Your karma has kept you in the cycle of incarnation and it will continue to do so if you don't do anything about it. If we understand that in every life we are the *result* of our karma, then the next question is: "Is this going to be repeated perpetually?" We create new karma now and add that to the old; we come down again to try to fix up the mess and again make new karma, which is again added to the old karma. This goes on life after life for the billions of human beings who obey the Law of Karma without *intelligence*. They continue to be influenced by circumstantial factors without any basic change in the pattern of their incarnations. To make a change you have to know what to change and why, and you have to know what the Plan for Humanity is and what the purpose of life is.

The Spiritual Path is designed to lift you out of this natural cycle of SAMSĀRA (the wheel of birth and death based on Reincarnation and Karma) to another region of the Universe, a higher dimension where you are not affected by Karma anymore. In other words, if you manage to reach the Buddhic dimension (attain Buddhic Consciousness) in this lifetime, you will cut out all of that karma. You 'de-programme' your computer; in fact, you unplug the whole works! You are no longer part of the great Law of Karma of *these* dimensions; you enter another Law of Karma relating to those higher—radically different—dimensions.

The Buddhic World is a world of absolute Unity, Bliss, Ecstasy,

Joy and Light, and beyond that are Nirvāṇa and other unimaginably beautiful worlds. Because of the Spiritual Path we know that these higher worlds exist, that it is possible to exist in a completely different way than how we live in this dimension, in the lower worlds. Shouldn't those worlds be the most desirable goal to achieve? Why not strive to reach those realms where there are infinitely more possibilities awaiting, possibilities for Intelligence, Love, Perfection, Joy and Bliss in infinite degrees? If you can choose the upper regions of the Cosmos, why would you want to keep circulating in the lower regions under the painful Law of Karma?

Now you have a new vision, a new purpose in your life to set out for Liberation, but you still have to deal with the karmic situation of the lower worlds (the Physical, Astral and Mental Worlds). You have to release yourself from your prison, from all those karmic forces and energies we have discussed, otherwise you cannot ascend to those higher kingdoms. This is where your understanding has to be very sharp. You know that you are still subject to the *old* Law of Karma (in *this* dimension), and that you have to align yourself with the *new* Law of Karma (in the Higher Worlds). You have to learn to neutralize the negative effect of the old karma that is holding you back so that you can reach those new realities.

At the same time you have to move step by step towards the state of Enlightenment, or Liberation, Self-Realization, Union with God, MOKṢA (Freedom of the Soul from birth and death), or whatever you like to call it. It is part of the Divine Plan that we should attain these higher states of consciousness and return to those higher dimensions—I say "return" because that is where Humanity originally came from (but that is another story). So we need to have the vision of our Liberation and Spiritual Perfection, and we have to know how to 'get there'. The unchangeable Law of Karma, however, will not make it easy. This is why meditation and spiritual practices alone are not enough. Unless your karma is neutralized, you won't get there.

Neutralizing Your Karmas

Let's start with this current lifetime. Of the three types of Karma—those you are creating now, those you are supposed to work out in this life and those you stored up previously—*the karmas you are creating now are the ones you have power over.*

Consider your physical, emotional and mental life. If you tend to think negatively or be in a negative emotional state or be physically abusive, then ask yourself, "Do I really want the karma of that?" If you don't want the negative karmic result then don't do it! It's as simple as that. There's no point doing something and becoming further enchained by karma, so start changing the way you think, feel and act, from this moment on, and try to avoid the negative consequences of karma on all levels—physical, emotional and mental. This means that you are already beginning to alter your future karma in a way that is partially liberating you in this lifetime.

In the same way, you know that good actions, emotions and thoughts will have good consequences. Doing so-called spiritual work and selflessly helping or serving others produce a lot of good karma for the future. For instance, meditation produces good karma; chanting together in a group produces very good karma; giving something away produces good karma; genuinely loving somebody produces good karma. In other words, all the things that you are taught to do in spiritual life are the very things that produce good karma, even if you don't understand the law behind it. You need to have a large amount of good karma to neutralize the bad karma and liberate yourself from its chains.

But this is only part of it; the other part is what to do with the karma that is supposed to be released in *this* lifetime. This is important because it is unavoidable.

Before you incarnated, you as a Soul chose to work through certain karma in this lifetime and you have to suffer through this; you can't do much about it, for the simple reason that you cannot go back on your word. You made an agreement with the *Lords of Karma* and it is written and sealed in the *Book of Life* (the Akashic Records: the history of every living being, planet or star that is written in the Divine Substance, Ākāśa). You cannot say, "Sorry, I've changed my mind." If the karma requires that you pay back or resolve some past situation by way of an accident in this lifetime, then you will have that accident. If your karma entails suffering a disease for ten or fifteen years, then you will have that disease.

There is a tendency in society to not accept suffering and pain because we think that it shouldn't exist. Still, in every spiritual or religious tradition, without exception, you are taught to *bear your cross* in this lifetime gracefully, happily, and joyfully, because you know it is the Will of God for you—in other words, you are working off that karmic account which you agreed to do as a Living Soul. You are then liberated from that karma; you can move and breathe more freely and have freedom to do spiritual work and live a spiritual life, and as a Soul you will have accomplished your purpose.

So there are two things you need to do to start neutralizing your karma:

First, you have to make sure, as much as you can, that you do the right thing *now*, in this lifetime, so that you don't accumulate negative karma for the future.

Second, you need to understand what karma you are supposed to be working out in this lifetime and not resist it.

If you can do this, you are beginning to be free in two areas: the future and the present. There only remains the stored-up karma that is still in your causal body.

Dealing with the Stored-up Karma

In the Buddhic World (the Fifth Kingdom or the Kingdom of God) there exists a special hierarchy composed of perfected human beings and their disciples and various orders of angelic beings dedicated to the Liberation of Humanity. This hierarchy is called the *Spiritual Hierarchy*, or the *Christ Hierarchy*, because the Christ is its Head.

If the Spiritual Hierarchy sees that you have made sufficient progress in your spiritual life, that you are genuine and sincere and that you are doing your utmost to change your lifestyle—you meditate, you are more loving and caring of others—*they will help*. They will do everything possible so that you will accomplish the whole karmic cycle in your lifetime, or in the after-death condition, in the Astral, Mental or Causal Worlds. In other words, if they see that a person has the potential to be liberated in their lifetime or the next, they will take upon themselves some of that person's stored-up negative karma which would otherwise be manifested, rather than delaying the Enlightenment process two, five or seven lifetimes.

This is not a process that applies to billions of people, only to those who are serious about the Spiritual Path and are world-servers, those who live their lives for the benefit of humankind and the world. If you are a world-server you can help the whole living process on this planet, so the Spiritual Hierarchy will do their part to help you—as a *gift* that comes under the Law of Forgiveness. This is the new law (also called the Law of Love) that Jesus brought in to take the place of the Old Testament law. It means: *the Compassionate Ones will neutralize your Karma if you are ready for it,* or if you are of such a nature that you will benefit the whole of Humanity. If the Spiritual Hierarchy sees that you are living a spiritual life and doing your utmost to help alleviate pain and suffering on this planet, if they see that "you glorify your Father with your good works" (Matthew 5: 16), they will give you a helping hand so that your Journey will be shorter and less painful.

If there were no help from the Spiritual Hierarchy, if we simply followed the Way of Nature, worked out our allotted karma and only accumulated a little bad karma in each life, we would still have to keep incarnating for many lives to clear the massive amount of *stored-up* karma. But thanks to the Law of Forgiveness there is a way to finally neutralize those remaining karmas.

Hopefully this will give you an understanding of how Karma affects your life and your journey on the Spiritual Path, and an inspiration to see things with a broader perspective, that everything is by plan and direction, everything has a reason, and if you understand and follow this you will get to your destination. ✷

Shadowland

CHAPTER 8

"Shadowland causes the suffering, war, evil, crime and hatred on this planet. It temporarily switches off the connection with the Inner Light, leaving a person in darkness to think, feel and do what he or she would never do while in a state of Connectedness."

For the vast majority of people the topic of Shadowland is incomprehensible; they have no idea about it whatsoever. But Shadowland is an important topic for everyone to understand. Then people won't be so judgmental of others or of Humanity itself. We will try to clarify this for you so that you develop a sense of compassion, because the only way you can understand real compassion is to understand the nature of Shadowland.

Shadowland concerns the idea of evil and why it exists. Remember, we're not talking philosophy. Philosophers will tell you their ideas of why evil exists, but those are just thought bubbles in their minds. You can philosophize about anything; it changes nothing except your mind. What we are talking about is an existential reality.

Imperfection is Inherent in All Things

Before any creation begins, whether it's the creation of a single human Soul or a hierarchy of beings or the creation of a planet, solar system or galaxy, it must have had a previous embodiment. Our Solar System is simply a re-embodiment, a reincarnation, of the Solar Logos from a previous time, after a previous Dissolution. The important point is that when anything restarts, it is not perfect; it is simply a replica of the last achievement of that embodiment in a previous lifetime.

Consider your present incarnation as a living Soul. If you have any sense of self-awareness you may have noticed that you are not perfect. The cause of your present imperfection is simply that in a previous lifetime, and in the many lifetimes before that, you weren't perfect. In your present life you manifest the total sum of qualities that you developed in all of your past series of incarnations. In other words, each life adds, subtracts or combines qualities, and then you are born again with the very last impression you created for yourself in your previous life. So right from the beginning you have had the handicap of imperfection.

If you extend this to a planetary scale, it is the same thing. Our planet, our Mother Earth, reincarnated from a previous planetary condition with the same imprint of whatever level she reached in that previous evolutionary field, and of course she too is imperfect. Our Solar Logos has had many embodiments. This particular one is simply the final point of evolution the Solar Logos attained at the end of its last embodiment, with the same particular qualities and lack of qualities. Of course, this can be extended to the galactic level and so on to the whole Cosmos itself. Everything incarnates according to previously established patterns, which become the starting point for the next incarnation. All this means is that imperfection is inherent in all things, and the ultimate cause or origin of Evil is imperfection.

When the Human Hierarchy was first created, it was created by four other Hierarchies who *themselves* were imperfect. Which means that they created our causal bodies as best they could, according to the previous attainment *they* themselves had. Another Hierarchy created our mental bodies, again as best they could, with the knowledge and understanding of the level of evolution they had reached. Another Hierarchy created our astral bodies, working also according to their knowledge and ability. The same Hierarchy created our etheric-physical body and the Physical Elemental Hierarchies produced our physical body. (Refer to the diagram *The Seven Great Planes of Being* at the front of this book.)

So four Hierarchies were involved in our creation on this planet at the beginning of time, and because all of them were imperfect, so was their creation imperfect. Our causal bodies weren't perfect, our mind bodies weren't perfect, our emotional bodies weren't perfect and our etheric and physical bodies weren't perfect. To compensate for that there is Evolution. In the first few million years Nature pushed us along an evolutionary line. Later on, once we had reached a certain level of self-consciousness, we had to do the best we could with our own evolutionary process.

We Have Made Earth a Dark Planet

Now because these things happened over millions of years, our imperfections created a deep groove or impression in the planetary aura, the invisible envelope that surrounds planet Earth. In other words, if we consider a few hundred million years of imperfect thoughts, imperfect feelings and imperfect activities by several billion entities, we should not be surprised that the subtle Light-Field around the planet has been warped. (We call this Light-Field the *Astral Light*, or the substance of the Astral World that was originally made of pure Light.) Over millions of years the wrong activity of the human family has warped and darkened the planetary aura until it has become a dark, murky sphere. We made Earth a dark planet, and it still is.

The Astral Light is not only of the Astral World but the total Light-Vibration from the causal dimensions through the mental dimensions, the astral dimensions and the etheric-physical and physical dimensions. It is a massive energy-field. And because we have warped it there are repercussions for us. Evil has become so embedded in the Astral Light that it is rebounding on us all the time. The negative force it generates continually circulates in Humanity, and so Humanity performs evil actions and thoughts—so much so that the Negative Force is actually increasing in strength rather than decreasing.

This is why it is difficult to overcome evil and why it takes real Soul-force to battle it. This is why the Buddha had to fight evil, or MĀRA, the force of evil in the world; why Jesus had to fight the devil; and why each of us will have to fight our battle when it is our appointed time. Each of us will have to face our crucifixion.

The average person just goes with the flow and is simply a victim of the Negative Force (the Negative Energy). Once you wake up to this and start to resist it, however, you will really have a battle on your hands. And when Humanity recognizes this en masse and starts fighting it with full force and full intelligence, there will be a huge battle because we have to neutralize aeons of wrong actions, wrong thoughts, wrong feelings and desires by billions of people that have been circulating and permeating through the planetary structure. It will be an inconceivable Armageddon.

The Negative Energy circulates throughout Humanity all the time, continually in touch with your physical body, your etheric-physical body (vital body), your astral body (feeling nature), your mind body (mind) and even your causal body (Soul). It is part of us and we are part of it. It is a snake-like movement of energy that weaves in and out of the entire planetary structure, which is why it is also called the *Great Serpent* or the *Serpent of Temptation* (the serpent that tempted Eve in *Genesis*).

What we are trying to say is that it's not an easy thing to solve evil and there is not much point blaming the government or God for it. Saying that God should know better or should do better is a silly idea that has nothing to do with reality. The reality is that God exists but there is one part of God Consciousness, the *Transcendental Consciousness* or the *Absolute Consciousness,* which is aloof; that is why it is called *transcendental.* It lives in a most indescribable reality of Absolute Light, Intelligence, Consciousness and Supernatural Perfection, but that is where it remains. And there is another part that, unfortunately, is imperfect.

It's like the Soul, which is also aloof. The Soul lives in the Causal World in a beautiful, harmonious, transcendental condition, full of Bliss and Light, and it has absolutely no interest in all the stuff happening down here on the personality level. These are just facts of nature, facts of life, how things are. You can philosophize about it anyway you like but it is not going to change anything.

Compassion and Forgiveness

Shadowland is circulating inside every one of us and sooner or later you will be touched by it. It is easy to point a finger at others and say, "That guy is a murderer or that guy did such a horrible thing. I am so holy that I am not capable of doing such a thing." You *are* capable of doing such a thing, and you did in your previous lifetimes. It's good for you that you are not involved at the moment, but it does not mean that you will not be involved in the future. The only way you can avoid it is by awakening to this understanding and forcing your Soul to engage in your affairs.

If you look at this from the point of view of Higher Consciousness you see it in a larger perspective. You see how the massive, seething Astral Light is impacting on Humanity, how the negative energy floods in and is released through one person or another, or simultaneously through one thousand people or one million people—which is why there are wars going on all the time. That is Shadowland.

So when you see or hear that someone has done something wrong you should be compassionate and send that person a wave of Love because that is the only thing that will help remedy the situation in the long run. If you add your own condemnation you just add another stream of negative energy, which reinforces the colossal Negative Force inherent in this planet. This is why Jesus, Buddha and all the great Teachers always taught *Compassion*. Forgive yourself, forgive your enemies, forgive those who do you wrong. The key word is always *forgive*, because in that forgiveness you release the negative mechanism and enable yourself to stay away from the imprint of those negative conditions.

Sometimes you read about a murderer who is executed after being on death row for many years. When I read that sort of story, rather than condemning the poor guy—I say "poor guy" but most people would say that he is an evil guy and should rot in hell—I am filled with an incredible pity for that person. Because it is true, he did do something wrong, but at the same time he did not do it. He was simply a victim of a tremendous force that he had no control over. (You might say that he did have a choice and could have *not* done it, but it doesn't work like that. You will see when it happens to you.) It is an irresistible force and it found an outlet through that person. Then he is punished by society for his "wrongdoing", being on death row for many years and then being executed. Can you imagine the anxiety that person goes through being on death row for so many years? That in itself adds to the suffering not only of that person but also of Humanity itself because when one human being suffers it reverberates on the rest of Humanity.

Most people live an isolated life. They shut out the world and are concerned only with their day-to-day affairs. Of course, if you shut out the whole world and nothing exists for you except your own little lifewave at that time, then you are not aware of suffering. But if you are a person who keeps up with the news and is aware of what is happening on the planet, the amount of human suffering will hit you.

So when we condemn people we are strengthening Shadowland, and that is what society does, again and again. It's what is called a vicious circle. We reinforce it by repeated wrong actions, creating a massive output of negative energy that rebounds on us. That is Shadowland.

Once you experience Shadowland within yourself, or get a glimpse of the horrible Evil that is gripping this planet, then—strange as it may seem—the sense of true Compassion arises inside you. From that moment on, all that you want to do is liberate yourself and liberate everybody else from the clutches of this Evil because you realize that human destiny cannot be good while we are endlessly recreating this negative situation for ourselves.

Rather than condemning someone you read about in the newspaper, you feel pity for that person. Of course, you feel pity for the victims as well, but your feeling of compassion does not extend only to the victims. On the contrary, it goes out more to the perpetrator of the act, because you can see the chain of events that caused the situation. So rather than blaming the evildoer, you understand that he is merely acting out a certain predestined course of events.

Instead of being quick to judge, therefore, be quick to forgive—including yourself. This is another point that is vital: you must not be harsh on yourself or self-critical. Simply remember that you are a victim of the Dark Force like everybody else. In fact, you can be entrapped by it even on the level of Buddhahood. You may say, "I thought when I reached Enlightenment I would have no problems anymore." If you say that, obviously, you haven't reached Enlightenment, because when you reach Enlightenment your problems become bigger. You will have more responsibility to bear and much more karma to work out. On the level of normal human consciousness you are just dealing with your own personal problems. On the level of Higher Consciousness you are dealing with the problems of Humanity. (And on the level of consciousness of the Buddha or the Christ, you are dealing with the problems of Cosmic Evil, the imperfect flow of energies between the various hierarchies on different evolutionary lines.)

But the point is to first forgive yourself. Most of us tend to hang onto our past wrongdoings, and that simply reinforces the Astral Light and allows the Dark Side of the Force to poison you. If you do not release a wrongdoing you add to the pool of wrong (negative) energy that is already there. So if you want to do the best thing for Humanity, forgive yourself and release what needs to be released so that you stay in your own clear Light.

Next, forgive anybody who ever did wrong to you. Look at all the people in your life who ever wronged you and just say, "They were under the influence of Shadowland" and send out a compassionate thought towards them. That is the only way we can overcome Shadowland; nothing will destroy it but Compassion. It will just keep percolating and circulating in our human consciousness until we wake up and become boundlessly compassionate. By clearing your consciousness of those who did any wrong to you, you are doing your part for the improvement of Humanity itself.

Now, what is Compassion? It is not a thought or an idea. Compassion is when your Soul sees evil, registers it and reacts to it by releasing a tremendous energy-wave of Love that comes out through you, the personality. That is why you can only become compassionate when you are Soul-Conscious and not before. The so-called love and compassion that people practise are mental ideas: God said to love your enemies, or Buddha said to love your fellow human beings, so people have a mental idea of compassion. This is not real Love, just an attempt at loving through a thought process. Real Love is an inner state of Higher Consciousness where you see the principle of Shadowland at work in yourself and in Humanity, and then the Soul responds to that recognition with a tremendous outpouring of Love, because that is the nature of the Soul. *The nature of the Soul is Love.*

In other words, each human being as a Soul is a totally loving being. There is not one Soul on this Earth that is not a loving Soul, because on the Soul level you are nothing but Love. (Similarly, the Transcendental Deity, which apparently is not engaged in anything on this planet, is Absolute Love.) So you cannot truly love until you are Soul-Conscious, and then it becomes automatic, a totally spontaneous energy welling up in your Heart and coming out of you.

Brothers of the Shadow

Another important point is that there are very few people who are consciously evil. Even the most vicious criminal, serial murderer, serial rapist or war criminal—even Hitler, Stalin or Idi Amin—is not consciously evil. Such a person is an ideal victim of Shadowland but it does not mean that he decides intelligently and consciously that he is going to do something evil with the full cooperation of his Soul, his *inner consciousness*. There is no such thing. What it means is that the Intelligence Principle in him has been blanked out, overcome by Shadowland, and he just acts out whatever he is doing. So he is not a *consciously* evil person; he is not even 'there' when he is committing his crimes.

But there *are* consciously evil people on this planet, although they are very few, and they are the *Dark Brothers* (also called the *Brothers of the Shadow* or the *Masters of the Dark Force*, among others). It is not easy to be one of them; being a serial murderer or a war criminal is not enough. You have to earn the right to become truly evil in this Cosmos. So who are the Dark Brothers?

Suppose for many lifetimes a person is a victim of Shadowland and he begins to enjoy it, becoming a person who performs evil for the sheer thrill and enjoyment of it. There are people on this planet at that stage who are moving onto the Dark Side of the Force. Such a person is still not a Dark Brother but he is moving in that direction. Now, before he can become a Dark Brother, however, he has to be challenged; his Soul has to be warned by the Hierarchy of Light.

In other words, suppose a person for many lifetimes does evil. The saving grace is still there for him and in one of his lifetimes his Soul will be approached by the Hierarchy of Light (the Light Side of the Force, if you like), who will give him the message to wake up because his personality, or his embodiment, is facing a real danger. The Soul then has to give momentary insight to the personality of that particular incarnation that what he is doing is wrong and will ultimately lead to a negative destiny. The personality, in other words, has to be given a chance to recognize his wrong actions.

If several of these warnings are given over several lifetimes and the personality continues to perform evil deeds, then there comes one final warning to the Soul and one final warning to the incarnated personality at that time. Now if that is not heeded the Light-Force withdraws and allows the person to become a Brother of the Shadow. Such people then slide into the irreversible condition that in Sanskrit is called AVĪTCI, which is the true Hell state from which there is no return. They have forever cut themselves off from the Forces of Light and cannot be redeemed until the end of this particular age.

Their redemption depends on what level of the Negative Hierarchy they have reached: If they have attained to a lesser degree on this Negative Path, they have to wait until the dissolution of the Earth, or PRALAYA, before they can be redeemed. If they attain to a greater degree of the Negative Side, they have to wait until the dissolution of the Solar System. If they have reached the Cosmic Hierarchy of Evil, they have to wait until the whole Universe withdraws from manifestation and restarts again.

This is portrayed in *Star Wars* when the hero realizes that his father is part of the Negative Hierarchy and tries to redeem him through compassion and love because he believes that there is still some good in him. This is possible if the person has not reached a high rank in the Hierarchy of Evil, but once they are confirmed to the Negative Path it is absolutely impossible to win them over. Any sense of love, mercy or forgiveness has been totally killed inside them. You can try to be as compassionate as you want but they will hate you even more for it. Your compassion will fuel their hatred because it is a vibration they cannot handle; it is actually a hurtful vibration for them, like burning them with fire. So they fight you even harder, throwing every force against you and doing whatever they can to destroy you.

But although those on the Dark Side of the Force are totally merciless, we must from our side still act compassionately and mercifully towards them. This seems really unfair but the reason is: if you don't act compassionately toward them, you will become like them. Your attitude towards them must be one of love, compassion and forgiveness because you realize that even they are victims of the Dark Force. The Hierarchy of the Dark Force are victims of themselves, because they would not be in that hierarchy unless they were victimized in the first place—by the *cosmic imbalance* that existed long before them. The original imperfection in the Cosmos created imperfect hierarchies that create imperfect conditions.

All the way back to the beginning of time, therefore, the key word is *imperfection*. If that had not been there all this evil would never have come into existence. Negative people and negative hierarchies would not exist; everything would be fine. So your compassion must be boundless, even for those who are committed to evil. It is the only right action for everyone.

Notice that those who work for the Light Force refer to the Dark Side as the *Brothers* of the Shadow. They refer to them as brothers, members of the same family. Even the most unimaginably evil person is your brother, part of your family. The fact is that the Forces of Light have a tremendous realization of the profound source of Evil.

Jesus said, "Evil will come but woe unto them through whom the evil comes" (Luke 17: 1). In other words, evil will come whether you like it or not, but pity the poor guys through whom it comes. "Woe unto them." Notice that He didn't say we should condemn them. Rather, be sorry for them. They are just victims of something beyond their control. Jesus was hinting that you have to be compassionate to the perpetrators of crime.

Thought-Power

Thought-Power is a complex topic and it ties in with Shadowland, Karma, Destiny and Evolution. So we'll start with a general understanding of the power of your thoughts, which has various aspects, and then we'll explain the practical application of this understanding so that we can use Thought-Power to positive ends.

When we first descended from the pure Spiritual Realms to the Causal Worlds as Living Souls, we didn't have feelings and had only a rudimentary thinking ability, which in Sanskrit is called CITTA-VRTTI, "movements of consciousness". But we could instantaneously register the results of those movements of consciousness, how they impacted on our environment and how the environment responded to them. In other words, through the sensory mechanism of the Soul we could sense the effects of the movements of our consciousness and their results.

We were then given mental bodies by the Solar Hierarchies and we began to think; we became a thinking entity—MANU, or "thinking man," the first human race of this planet. At that time, because we had no emotional or physical bodies, we could see the results of our thoughts because we could still function with about eighty percent of the internal sensory mechanism of the Soul. Whenever we released a thought we could immediately see its result in our environment—the Mental World, the world of thought.

Millions of years later, we became embodied in astral bodies, which are feeling bodies. Once enmeshed in our astral bodies, we were disconnected from the thought realm and could no longer see or sense the result of our thoughts. We had descended onto another level and had become astrally conscious, aware of the Astral World as one massive sea of feelings and emotions, but we had lost touch with the thinking principle. Although we were still able to think, we could not perceive the effects of those thoughts. And this is where we first lost the awareness of the divine power of thought within us.

Finally, about three million years later, we assumed etheric-physical bodies and then dense animal physical bodies. The astral body, etheric-physical body and physical body are three intermediary layers that cover our thought processes, so we have completely lost touch with what thought is. We are still thinking beings but we cannot feel the impact of every thought we make, how it affects others and how it rebounds on us.

This is a disaster, unfortunately, because we actually produce our life through Thought-Power. Moment by moment, day by day, year by year, lifetime by lifetime, we direct our life through Thought-Power, but because we do not see the immediate effects of our thoughts, we do not understand the awesome implications of that power. And this is why Mankind is in such a disastrous situation on the planet. People are continually thinking wrong thoughts because they are oblivious to the effects of those wrong thoughts. If they could see their effects, they would stop thinking them.

We Are Creators

Over the last one hundred years or so there have been many so-called positive thought schools that have developed, mainly in English speaking countries, because people realize that the power of thought is important in order to improve their lives. But there's more to it than that. Positive thought is an excellent idea but there is an esoteric reason why we should understand the power of positive thought more deeply. The reason is that we are actually *creative beings*.

In the scheme of evolution for our Solar System, there are twelve Creative Hierarchies, some of whom, as was mentioned previously, created our various bodies. Humanity is called the *Fourth Creative Hierarchy*, but the numeration is of no importance here. What is important is that we are classed as a *creative* hierarchy, and we are creative even as our Creators were creative. The only difference is that we create by Thought-Power, the ability of our minds to formulate something and embody it in a form, whereas the other hierarchies use other energies and powers.

We are essentially Divine Creators, literally gods and goddesses, although we are *un*conscious creators at this stage. Every time we think a single thought it creates a shape or a form in our mental body— a *thoughtform*. More importantly, that thought is not just an empty form; it is *alive* with the intelligence, the consciousness and the power of the person who produced it. So every thought you make produces a form with a certain amount of life in it, with your own intelligence and understanding, your own life-current and energy behind it. And because those thoughts are alive they modify your consciousness. This means that if you keep thinking a thought over and over again, that thoughtform begins to increase in size, becoming infused with more energy and power, until it takes over your whole mental body. If it is a negative thought, it can eat away at you like a cancer and warp your view of reality.

The Negative Power of Thought

Having a prejudice against certain races or nationalities, for example, builds a powerful thoughtform in your auric field that can become an all-consuming idea, to the point of paranoia. You then fashion your life according to it, living your whole life from the angle of that thoughtform, and every judgement you make is that thoughtform put into action. Unfortunately, you may be prejudiced against or conditioned by many things, which means you have many thoughtforms that completely cloud your vision of reality.

Incidentally, "your vision of reality" includes your thoughts about yourself. Believe it or not, you can have a cancerous thought about yourself: when you have low self-esteem, for example. Some people have a very bad self-image and carry a strong thoughtform inside themselves that they are good for nothing, that they are hopeless and cannot make it in life, and so on. It is a living thoughtform in their auric field and they continually act it out.

Now, these living thoughtforms are very real and they warp not only the way you look at life but also the way you relate to other people. You can have cancerous thoughtforms toward others—maybe people you know or people belonging to a certain race, culture, religion or country that you have a fixed view about. Every time you see such a person a thoughtform automatically tells you that they are no good, even if you don't even know them. You cannot communicate normally with that person because you 'know' he or she is no good, because the thoughtform within you tells you that, and no other possibility can exist but that thought.

That's how it is with fundamentalists, whether they are Christian, Muslim, Jewish or whatever. Fundamentalist Christians, for example, think that every other group or individual who is not of their church is of the devil; every other teaching not from their own particular local church is of the devil; scientists and others who do not believe exactly the same thing they do are of the devil. They approach life through this colossal thoughtform, which completely wipes out any intelligence in their consciousness when dealing with other people outside of their group. Of course, there are fundamentalists in philosophy, politics science, art—in every area of life. Their thoughts are locked into a pattern and they cannot see beyond it and will not accept anything beyond it.

Naturally, such thoughts may have been generated by, and inherited from, your parents. Most prejudices come from parents and relatives, or the religion or culture you are brought up in, and they are usually inherited through association with people who have those prejudices. In many cases you absorb them as a child and recreate them in your own system, and then you really believe in them. As a child, without the ability to question, you tend to accept things. Once you have accepted a thought, it becomes its own living reality inside you, with its own life and its own power to guide you (or more precisely, *misguide* you) through the rest of your life. This is what you need to understand about Thought-Power.

Besides the thoughts you generate over this lifetime, however, there are the thoughts you generated over your many past lifetimes, which are waiting for you in Shadowland. In other words, you pick up not only the prejudices you inherit in this lifetime but also the thoughtforms in Shadowland from your own past lives, which will come back to you. This is because when you 'die' in this life you just leave your physical body; you carry with you your mind, which remains with you in the after-death condition. So the thoughtforms you generated in every one of your many incarnations are added to your 'account' in Shadowland.

Suppose in a past life two thousand years ago you were prejudiced against the Greeks. That prejudice built up a cancerous thoughtform in your aura in that lifetime. When you died you dropped your physical body but that prejudice against the Greeks remained in your mind, reserved for you in Shadowland. And when you come back into incarnation it is given back to you and it will infiltrate your aura, your mental body, with the same negative, devastating effects. In other words, your mind is already warped even before you are born, and then all the negative thoughtforms you generate are added on. So you have to deal with the thoughtforms you generate and those that remain connected to you from your past lives.

Thought-Power, Shadowland and Karma

Another aspect of Thought-Power is the ability to release thoughts. This is something that is quite common yet most people do not know about. What happens if you have been thinking of a person with prejudice and you do it over and over again? We have seen that if you do that just once you generate a thoughtform in your aura that stays there and poisons your own mental body. But if you think that thought many times it becomes so powerful that it becomes an independent entity—what we call a *Thought-Elemental*—infused with its own life, its own energy and its own reality derived directly from you. That elemental then breaks away from your auric field and travels to the person concerned, attaches itself to their auric field and acts on their mental body. Suddenly that person will feel depressed or angry and cannot figure out why.

This is not a unique event; it happens every day and we do it all the time. And the danger in it is real, that is to say, we can actually ruin other people's lives by thinking negatively about them. This is why there is a rule in spiritual life: If you know that somebody did something wrong, keep quiet, don't gossip about it, because all you are then doing is amplifying it, causing it to rebound on that person even worse. And if you know that somebody other people are gossiping about is innocent, then defend that person.

The normal tendency when somebody does something wrong is to broadcast it. Everybody discusses it, adds their thoughts to it and amplifies it until it grows out of proportion and feeds the power that Shadowland has over all Humanity. So you should keep silent; it's none of your business, it's that person's karma to work out. By remaining silent you do not feed that negative energy current, you do not give power to the Opposition, to Shadowland, the storehouse of evil that already exists. And if there is somebody you know who is being attacked, put every positive thought you can in defence of that person because then you are increasing the power of Light in that person, as well as in the world. Remember, there's no such thing as a totally bad person; every person is a living Soul and every person has Light in them.

Now, once a thought gets out of your control, which it does when it's strong enough, you cannot recall it. Suppose you say to yourself everyday that you hate a certain person or group of people. Then, as I said, that thoughtform detaches itself from you and starts attacking that person or group, whoever is the focal point of your hatred. Unfortunately, the matter does not end there because *you* are incurring

karma by doing this, whether you are aware of it or not. You are re-
sponsible for that thoughtform, and there will be karmic consequences
of your action.

Most people think that *karma* refers to the results of physical actions only; they don't appreciate that thoughts are also actions. *Thinking is acting.* Thoughts are a more subtle form of matter but they have
the same karmic consequences as physical actions. If you hit somebody
physically, you will probably get a reaction from that person, and you
will understand the Law of Karma, action and reaction. Many people,
however, think that there is no consequence of thinking evil or wrong
of somebody, but the results of such thoughts will rebound on you,
sooner or later, because the principle is exactly the same.

This is why all the great Teachers always emphasized forgiveness,
forgiving yourself and others. If you can't forgive another for doing
wrong to you, or you can't forgive yourself for doing wrong to somebody else, then the action-reaction principle keeps circulating—inside
you, between the people concerned and within the planet. You're just
adding fuel to the fire all the time. This is why the Law of Love is
absolute and the primary way to be in the world.

Another aspect of Thought-Power to consider is what happens
when negativity comes to you from somebody else. There may be some
people who don't like you and decide they want to hurt you. This is
quite common in the world; people are filled with hate. Now what
happens in this case is that by hating you they are naturally warping
their own mind, putting poison into their own auric field, and when
that poison becomes strong enough because they keep feeding it with
hate towards you, that thought will come out of themselves, travel
towards you, and start working on you to hurt you. You can actually
feel it: it's like you're swamped by a tremendous black cloud and sud-

denly find yourself in darkness. It is far worse if this is done by a group of people. The group's thoughtform becomes immensely powerful and it can be devastating for the individual concerned. Most people do not have the skill to fight it, so they succumb to a physical or mental illness or other effect.

This is why it is so important to have this knowledge; with it, you can understand what is happening and try to avoid the negative effects.

The Positive Power of Thought

The third aspect of Thought-Power is the positive application of thought. So what happens when thought is used positively? When you meditate or chant, you create positive thoughtforms, and these positive thoughts have the same laws operating behind them as negative thoughts. If you generate positive thoughts on your own, they will energize your auric field in a *positive* way: they will give you happiness, peace, joy and a feeling of well-being. When a group of people does this, the Light-energy of the group is increased along the line of the spiritual activity the group is doing. And, like negative thoughts, positive thoughts can build up in a person until they break away from the person's auric field and affect somebody else who is able to register them. Similarly, a group of people chanting, meditating or using positive affirmations creates a huge thoughtform that breaks away from the group and affects individuals or other groups able to register that vibration.

Through the positive use of Thought-Power, therefore, we can energize and restructure our own reality and that of another person's in beneficial ways, and a group can restructure its own reality and the world reality, by putting a positive vibration into the environment.

This is the idea behind so-called *absent healing*. To the ancients there were two kinds of healing: healing through physical touch and healing from a distance, which was conveyed by Thought-Power. The ancient healers would first align themselves to the Soul Realm through meditation and then create a healing thoughtform in their mind and consciously send it to the person to be healed. It worked then and it still does today. It is a conscious, intelligent way of using Thought-Power.

A practical application of this is that if you know somebody who is feeling depressed or is sick or is having some difficulty in life, send positive thoughts to that person, rather than dwelling on the negative side of the situation and feeding the negative energy currents. Imagine that person surrounded by light, radiantly happy, and send that thought out to them and help them heal or improve their circumstances. Do this because you know you are a creator and your thought is alive and it can *do* things. This is the magic part of it—your thought is a living entity and you can send it forth and it will do its work.

Society is continually feeding Shadowland with negative thinking and therefore perpetuating it. If everybody stopped providing it with negative attention, it would explode into nothing because Shadowland is actually nothing. It is simply the mass of negative thoughts that we have about each other and about all kinds of things, and it would not exist without them. The point is that Thought-Power has a negative aspect and a positive side and they both work according to the same principle. So rather than allowing the negative aspect to dominate you, you should work on consciously using the positive aspect of Thought-Power.

The Law of Love & Forgiveness

So it is important to be aware of the power of your thoughts for both good and bad, and then try to use that power only for good, only for that which brings in the Light, so that you help the Light Principle—

not the Shadowland—in you and in the world. Christ said, "You are either for me or against me" (Matthew 12: 30). There is nothing in between. You are either working for the wrong side or for the right side. You cannot fluctuate between working for the Light and working for the Darkness.

Remember, Shadowland is not real; it's a shadow. Light is real; it's a permanent substance. All the negative stuff that goes on in the world is not real, until we feed it, until *we make it real* in our own consciousness.

As we mentioned previously, when you die, the only thing you take with you is your mind. Your physical body, etheric-physical body and astral body will perish, but *you*—the thinking, intelligent being that you are—remain unchanged in the after-death condition. Therefore, whatever you are when you die is that which remains. If your mind is filled with hateful, negative thoughts before you die, that is what you take with you. If your mind is filled with loving, harmonious thoughts, that is what you take with you.

Being aware of this, therefore, try to disengage from any negative thoughts, no matter where they come from. If they come from you, then stop them; if they come from another person, disengage from them; if they come from society, do not feed and perpetuate them. You don't have to be swamped by evil; you can stand in your own Light and send out positive energy. You have that choice all the time.

Ultimately, your whole life will be summarized when you die, at what we call the *Moment of Reckoning* or the *Moment of Judgement*, when you stand in the Light of your Soul and the Soul instantly judges your incarnation, its weaknesses and strengths. After that, there is nothing you can alter. So the state of your consciousness at the moment of death is supremely important in determining your future—not only your future in the after-death conditions (the heaven or hell worlds you will experience) but how you will be reborn, under what circumstances and with what karma to work out, or whether you can stand free as a Liberated Soul and not have to reincarnate at all.

This is where the Law of Love and Forgiveness comes in, because it is important that when you die you are not carrying any burden with you. So reflect on what we have said and look inside you. If you hate or dislike somebody or have a grudge against somebody, just let it go. Release that energy, that thought mechanism in your mind. Forget it. Let it out of your consciousness through the act of forgiveness. At that moment you break a karmic link with that person, and you release that person from any debt owing you. You have let it go, so there is no action or reaction possible after that. You have freed that person, and you have freed yourself.

Remember that the best aspect of Thought-Power is that you can heal and transform yourself and others through Thought-Power; you can do miracles through Thought-Power. This is the positive application of it, and you can do it by formulating and sending out positive, loving thoughts to others. First, realize that you are a living Soul full of joy and bliss, a creator by thought, and then create a beautiful thoughtform, a real elemental being vibrating with life, energy, love and dynamism, and send it out to someone.

We are creators, but unfortunately we are usually not conscious of it. Of course, it's not possible that we can be one hundred percent conscious of our thoughts all the time. But by reflecting on our thoughts from time to time when we have a quiet moment, we will find that our awareness of Thought-Power will increase. Then, we will be able to work the magic of Thought-Power in a transformative, miraculous way, whenever we want.

God is hidden within you and in all men, women and children.
Search within yourself and find out.

Christ is a fact. The Christ is Light.
God is a fact. God is Light.
Truth is a fact. Truth is Light.

Ultimately the Light will swallow up the Darkness,
And Evil shall be no more. ⚡

Imre Vallyon,
Heavens & Hells of the Mind (2007) i. 228.

God the Mother

CHAPTER 9

"When we awake internally to the idea that we are more than what we appear to be, that we have to follow a spiritual path, it is She calling us—because She is us. Then, when we start following that call, the aid will come from Her unasked. We don't have to pray to Her; all we need will be given to us, and more."

If you have been brought up in any of the three Western religions—the Jewish, Christian and Muslim religions—you know that they are basically male-oriented religions. They can only think of the Deity as a male god. In Christianity there is the Father, who is male; the Son, who is male; and the Holy Spirit, who is also male. In the Muslim religion there is just one God, who is male, and, of course, in the Jewish religion God is also male. Consequently, the hundreds of millions of people who have been brought up or are being brought up today in these three Western religions are fed with the idea that God is male, and that's it.

As a result, the ecclesiastical hierarchies of these religions are also male. The Jewish rabbis are male, the Muslim mullahs and church authorities are male, and the Christian priests are all male. The Anglican Church is an exception as it does allow female priests or representatives of God, but that wasn't the original idea of the Christian Church. So the idea that there is a femaleness in the Cosmos has been obliterated in these religions, which concentrate on the masculine expression in their theologies, in their thinking about reality, and in their priestcraft and practices.

In the Eastern religions, however, there is a great emphasis on the balance between male and female polarities, like Yin and Yang in the Chinese religions and the gods and goddesses in the Tibetan, Buddhist and Hindu religions, where it's quite normal for each god to have a corresponding goddess. So the idea that you can worship a female deity in conjunction with a god, or go straight to a female deity for Enlightenment, is quite normal in the Eastern religions. They understand that the Female has all kinds of powers and they can invoke a female deity for material, psychic or spiritual purposes.

The Western religions, however, do not have this idea that you can approach Reality through a female ideal. Because of the total concentration on the masculine side, the Western consciousness does not know that there is a female side, that there are feminine powers that can be awakened, and so it would be quite abnormal for them to start worshipping a female deity.

The Feminine Aspect in Western Consciousness

It is interesting to look back at the history of the Roman Catholic Church and see how, over many centuries and without any real understanding on the part of the authorities, the Church unconsciously introduced the Female idea.

First of all, there was Jesus, who was the Christ and was considered to be a Divine Incarnation. About two hundred years after the death of Jesus, the Church Fathers, who had not given much thought to the mother of Jesus, started wondering how a Divine Incarnation could be born to an ordinary mortal female, and they built up a complicated, tortuous theology around the thinking that if Jesus was a Divine Incarnation, then naturally the mother of that Divine Incarnation—Mary, or Miriam—must have been a special person.

So they decided that she wasn't really a normal human but a special incarnation, as she had been chosen to bring Jesus the Christ into the world. So they lifted her one step higher and she became a unique reality unto herself, no longer part of the normal male-female human species but a special embodiment that was able to produce the Divine Incarnation. Then, because Mary died of natural causes, they thought that she obviously could not just go to heaven like every other woman, so they decided that she must have *ascended*, been lifted up by Divine Grace.

For a couple of centuries the church authorities were happy with Mary's status, but then they started thinking, "Okay, if she ascended to Heaven, what is she doing there? What is her relationship to the Father, who sits on a throne in Heaven, and to Jesus, who sits on another throne?" So they decided to give her a throne of her own and she became the Queen of Heaven. Later, they realized that as the Queen of Heaven she must have power and authority, so they gave her rulership over the angelic and human hierarchies, and she became the Queen of the Angels and the Queen of Human Beings.

This is why the Roman Catholic Church says that you can pray to the Virgin Mary and she will do things for you. Now, I think this is rather exploitive. Imagine eight hundred million Roman Catholics praying to the Virgin Mary every day, one praying for a car, one for a son, another for a new wife or husband, another for a new trinket, another for a new job. Logically, this is impossible; even if she heard the prayers she would be kept busy trying to organize everybody's karma and circumstances to fulfil their desires. It's the wrong conception of what the Feminine Principle is about.

So we started with Miriam, a humble village woman from Israel and the mother of Jesus, who became further and further exalted until she became the Queen of Heaven and someone to whom we could pray for favours. And nowadays, of course, the Roman Catholics still worship her as the Queen of Heaven. But what is wrong with this picture? Why did this idea develop in such a warped way?

What the Church did over these eleven or twelve hundred years was to re-establish the truth that the Ancients knew: *there is a Divine Feminine in the Cosmos that has always been in existence.* But because they could not openly say that this power existed before the time of Christ, they had to do a tortuous manoeuvre of lifting a human female and giving her all these degrees and powers. Actually, Mary was just a mortal human, a highly advanced spiritual disciple, but she certainly was not the great ŚAKTI, the great Universal Power, the great Mother of the Cosmos, who has always been in existence and from whom the whole Cosmos has come into being.

If you are a Roman Catholic, it is important to understand that this idea of worshipping Mary came about in a contorted way and that it is not a new idea at all. In actuality, the Feminine was worshipped in all the ancient religions and, what is more, there were women in the priestcraft—priestesses in Rome, Egypt, Greece, India, China, Tibet and all over Asia. The Roman Catholic Church is still struggling with the idea of priestesses. Since the 1960s theologians have been trying to shift the idea of Mary the Queen of Heaven a bit further, to make it more universal, and they have been trying to convince the Pope that the Church should have priestesses doing the same things that the priests do. But at this stage, the Church has still refused to do that. That would be too much of an expansion because if there were priestesses that would mean that God is also a Goddess, which is something that the Church cannot yet accept.

But it is the same with the Muslim religion: it would be absolutely impossible to convince them there is a Feminine Principle. And it is the same with the Jewish religion: it's unimaginable that they would switch from the male God to a female Goddess idea. At least, the Roman Catholic Church has gone partway toward the right idea, although they are still far behind.

If you understand that there is a Universal Feminine that is not a human being called Mary but a cosmic principle stretching throughout all Creation—inside you and outside you, within the various realms of the Universe—then you will understand that it is possible to pray to Her. You would not be praying to one little creature but to a universal principle, a vast cosmic reality, an infinite ocean of consciousness, intelligence, energy, bliss, possibility and power. Then, you wouldn't have to bother poor old Mary, who is trying to settle down in Heaven.

So it's important for Westerners first to accept that there is a Universal Goddess, or a female aspect of God—God the Mother—and then figure out what to do with that knowledge, how to relate to that female aspect.

The Feminine Aspect in the Cosmos

Another understanding of the Feminine Reality is that of the new-agers who think it has something to do with worshipping goddesses from Egyptian, Greek or Roman myths, or stones, plants, energy currents, the moon or Mother Earth. Natural religions such as pagan and shamanistic religions existed all over the continent of Europe in ancient days, as well as in places like Mongolia, Tibet, China, Japan and other parts of the world where there were no major religions—what I call *high-frequency religions*—like Buddhism, Hinduism or Christianity. Shamanistic and pagan religions usually tune into Nature in its visible, tangible form—a real animal, a real tree, a real rock, the physical moon or a physical place on Earth. It is the worship of Nature in its densest (material) form.

Now this is also a warped idea of the Goddess, because it *limits* the Goddess to a very small expression. Of course, the Goddess *is* in a stone, a tree, an animal, the moon and the planet Earth but this conception is limited because it is only looking at little fragments of Her, instead of the extraordinarily large Absolute Reality that the real Feminine is: PARAŚAKTI, which means the Supreme Power, the Supreme Feminine, that which is omnipotent, omniscient, and omnipresent throughout all of Space. *That* is the Great Goddess. And it is important that we do not identify Her totality with only little aspects and parts of Her. So the New-Age thinking has to be cleared away and we have to clarify in the Western consciousness that the Feminine is actually an *infinite possibility*.

There are two aspects in Creation: the Male and the Female, and it is important not to limit these aspects. People tend to identify with what they already know, such as the human female or the human male, but for us to understand the Male Principle (the Divine Father) and the Female Principle (the Divine Mother), they have to be brought down to the physical level. In the old days, the mother used to rule the household (and she still does in many households). She looked after the children, cooked the meals, told the husband what to do and what not to do. In the Cosmos, the Divine Mother rules all the realms from the Physical Creation all the way up to Nirvāṇa, which include the Astral Creation, the Mental Creation, the Causal Creation and the Buddhic Creation (the subtlest part of the Material Creation). The Planes of Being from Nirvāṇa and above are the domain of the Male, the Divine Father.

The Divine Mother Works for Our Salvation

The Divine Mother, the Great Feminine, has only one interest: the total evolution of the entire Universe. In other words, the Universe came out of Nirvāṇa aeons ago and the task of bringing all the worlds back to Nirvāṇa is the job of the Mother. It's like in the old days when it was the mother's job to educate the children and tell them what to do and how to live. In the Animal Kingdom it has always been that way; the mother teaches her young about life. This is a reflection in the physical world of how PARAŚAKTI, the Divine Mother, teaches all the hierarchies in all of Manifested Creation so that they can become enlightened and return to the Source from which they came.

That is the function of the Mother but you have to understand that She has a way of doing things according to a cosmic plan. In Her Cosmic Mind, She knows that certain evolutionary species, like the angelic, human, animal and elemental species, go through a schooling process, and She takes them through that systematically, over billions and billions of years.

She also has inside Her another blueprint, for what I call *hastened evolution*. This means that certain species can access Her powers and energies on a much higher level, thereby attaining Enlightenment quicker than through natural evolution, which takes billions and billions of years. The sub-human kingdoms—the Animal Kingdom and the Elemental Kingdom—cannot do that. But humans, angels and higher orders of entities can link up to special patterns within Her Cosmic Mind and through those patterns hasten their own evolution and unfoldment.

For us humans, therefore, the way to hasten our evolution is to understand *first* that She exists, *second* that She has the keys to higher possibilities, and *third* that we have to start using those keys and awaken our connection to Her on that higher level.

All Forms Emanate from Her Sounding-Light Nature

The Great Goddess responds to Sound; in fact, She is Sound, Sounding-Light Vibration. When you listen internally, you can hear Her music, which is the Creative Power, the Creative Sound by which She creates the Buddhic World, the Causal World, the Mental World, the Astral World, the Etheric World and the Physical World. In Her domain, Light and Sound are one—where there is a sound, there is light with it, and where there is light there is sound with it; the two are inseparable.

All *forms* come out of Her Sounding-Light nature. The Buddhic World is like a sea of luminous, homogenous "matter". In the Causal World that sea turns into streams of Sounding-Light energies that are not homogenous. In the Mental World those streams of energy take shapes—triangular shapes, cubic shapes, all kinds of geometric shapes. The Astral World has recognizable human shapes, animal shapes and even flower, plant and tree shapes. And the Physical World has the most diversity of shapes. Even the densest physical object is made out of the Sounding-Light Current, which is the Great Śakti, the Divine Power that is in everything. But She is not just *in* everything; She *is* everything!

This is the biggest key, if you can understand it: She is you. She is the world. She is this Creation. It's not as if She looks down upon Creation and changes things here and there. She is actually changing Herself. She is not only the process of change but the thing being changed. She is all the processes and all the substances in all the realms up to Nirvāṇa, and everything is Her own movement within Herself.

Her Plan is to Evolve All Life

If you understand this one single idea, you'll become liberated very quickly. In the past, people meditated and did spiritual practices for their own Enlightenment, their own evolution or glorification. But in actuality, whatever we do it is the Goddess doing it within Herself, for Herself.

And what is more, She is doing it because it is part of Her great Cosmic Evolutionary Plan. She has a plan for every solar system and every planet in the Cosmos, including ours. She wants us to be enlightened, regardless of whether we want it or not! And She will bring that about. Every living creature will be enlightened by the appointed time. She is steadily working out Her Plan aeon after aeon until it is fulfilled. Her vision is vast but She is *irresistible*.

Once you have seen a glimmer of Her Plan in Higher Consciousness, you realize what the Mother wants you to do, why you have to meditate, why you have to overcome the limitations within yourself, because you can see how Her Plan is working. And then you cooperate with it. To cooperate with Her is the most joyous thing you can do because you realize how amazing Her Plan is. Not only that, it becomes your responsibility to teach it to others. That's why the truly enlightened Teachers have always taught; they could not imagine not teaching because it would be totally and utterly irresponsible.

Suppose you are driving a car and you stop in front of a precipice. If a car is coming behind you, you feel that it is your responsibility to stop the other car so that it doesn't plunge into the precipice. When you have seen Her Plan, it's like that. Not only do you realize that the Divine Mother is working toward the evolution of the Universe, and pushing you toward a higher expression of yourself, but you also realize that it is your responsibility to follow Her, and to warn others to follow Her because you see where the dangers are if they don't.

You realize that knowledge is salvation, the only thing that will help you follow that divine pattern. You then become a natural teacher, conveying what you know inside to help others achieve the same knowledge. And it is not you at all, for you are simply following the great desire of the Divine Feminine.

She Will Give You Everything You Need To Fulfil Your Part of the Plan

So when we awake internally to the idea that we are more than what we appear to be, that we have to follow a spiritual path, it is She calling us—because She is us. Then, when we start following that call, the aid will come from Her unasked. We don't have to pray to Her; all we need will be given to us, and more.

It's only when people are in the state of spiritual ignorance, when they are still in the worldly consciousness, that they think they are separated from the Divine and they have to pray to the Deity for things. [3] But once you are working with Her to establish the Divine Plan within you and in the world, you don't need to ask for anything. Everything you need will come to you because you are working for Her Plan, with Her Plan, and She will give you what you need to fulfil your part of the Plan. Remember, your part is only a small part of a larger part; nevertheless, She will give you all the things you need to fulfil your part, your destiny, what *you* have to do as part of the great Divine Plan.

It is therefore important that you do not think of the Goddess as something "out there", or as a historical figure like the Virgin Mary or Quan Yin or Isis, or as a stone or the moon. I want you to realize that the Goddess is already inside you; in fact, it is you who is on the outside. In Higher Consciousness you realize that it is you, not the Divine, who is disconnected. The Divine cannot be disconnected from itself; it's everywhere. Once you connect inside and realize that everything is one, you will be able to sense the Plan and to sense how She works inside you and guides you like a mother—at times indirectly, giving you subtle feelings of what you should and should not do, and at times directly, warning you of danger or something that is wrong in your environment. But at all times She will guide you in what I call your *destiny line*.

---

3 The Divine Mother does not want people to be in a state of ignorance; it actually gives her pain, quite literally. If you tune into Her Cosmic Mind, you will find a region of extreme pain inside Her, which exists because so many people on this planet are doing the wrong thing—thinking, feeling and acting in ways that are not in harmony with Her Cosmic Vibration, which is pure and clear and in tune with Reality. Therefore, when billions of people are putting out the wrong energy waves into the Cosmos, She picks them up and they become a tremendous suffering for Her.

Your Karma and Your Destiny

Once you have direct contact with the Goddess within you, your destiny line becomes clear. For instance, one day you may wake up and know that there is some higher possibility, a higher purpose, what you need to do in this lifetime—call it Self-Realization or the knowledge of God, Truth, Nirvāṇa or the Kingdom of Heaven. In that moment you realize your destiny line in this lifetime. The vision always has to be a spiritual one, toward the final fulfilment of human destiny, and it may come to you when you are young or during middle age or old age. But it will come to you sometime and then it will be clear to you that you have a great destiny to fulfil. But with that, of course, comes the karma you bring over from previous lifetimes.

The average person's destiny is mixed up with his or her karma because of past negative actions, and even people on the Spiritual Path have a lot of negative karma to work through. So it is easy for them to get confused about what is their destiny line and what is their working out of karma. They don't understand that Karma is one thing and the destiny line is something completely different; they don't understand that there is a single, clear destiny line in one's life that one follows no matter what their karma may be.

The karma (which usually comes from a past life and your present life) will knock you left and right and all over the place, one disaster after another. Of course, when you're dealing with karma day after day, the vision that you have of your great destiny in this lifetime becomes more and more blurred until the day comes when you are so involved in your karma that you completely forget your destiny line. This is when many people leave the Spiritual Path. When you see them again years later, they are still the same as they were before. They have not changed because their destiny line has been suspended while they have been struggling with their karma.

Now this is really a disaster because what it means is that as a Soul you had a vision, you tuned in and understood what your Plan was in this lifetime, but as a personality you got swamped by your karmic circumstances. So you suspend your Soul vision and live your life totally as a personality, dealing with all your personality stuff and completely forgetting your Soul vision for this lifetime, which is your real destiny line.

You have to understand that just because you sense your Soul vision it doesn't mean that you will not have to work out your karma on the personality level—because of the Law of Karma. We have a vast backlog of karma from thousands of previous lifetimes, and unfortunately, with the way the Universe is and the way the Spiritual Path is, we have to follow the Soul (destiny) line and the personality (karmic) line, and somehow deal with the two simultaneously. Otherwise, we just stagnate and fail life after life. So in this lifetime, you have to keep your Soul vision, your destiny, clear and at the same time deal with your karma as it comes along.

Here, too, the power of the Divine Feminine can help: She strengthens the vision of your destiny line and gives you power over your karma, helping to neutralize it or lessen its effects. Karma is like an ocean, with one wave pushing the water and creating another wave. Once started, the waves keep coming until they are neutralized. Now, if you put a concrete wall in the path of a wave, it will bash against the wall and won't go anywhere. Well, when we have connected with the Feminine through meditation on one of Her mantras, we introduce a wall of energy that blocks the motion of karma. If the wall is stronger than the karma, it can block the karma altogether; if the karma is stronger, the wave will go over the wall but not with its full power.

Using the Feminine Energy, therefore, will change your life, how your personality line is going to work out. Sometimes, of course, the karma is very strong; but even then the aftereffects will be less drastic. It's hard to explain but let's put it this way: Suppose you are suffering from cancer. If you are not following your spiritual destiny in tune with the Feminine Power, if you are an ordinary human being with only a personal view of life, naturally you will begin to feel sorry for yourself. But if you are living a spiritual life in tune with the Feminine, the Divine Mother, you will understand that the disease is the result of karma and that it does not change your spiritual destiny. You know that no disease or natural disaster has the power to change your spiritual vision, the essential Self-nature within you.

So if you live like that and take whatever karma comes and work it out, doing your best under the circumstances, no karma can stop you from realizing your spiritual destiny. Even the greatest Saints— Christian, Muslim, Hindu or Buddhist—had physical diseases and problems. But they accepted them and did not let them get in the way of their spiritual destiny. An example of how spiritual destiny and physical karma relate is the life of a great Saint in India who died at a young age of a heart attack. In his life he did everything correctly: he was a pure vegetarian and never had aggressive or violent thoughts or moods. He had no quality that you could blame him for and say he deserved to die of a heart attack at a young age. But he did, because of his past karma. Nevertheless, it did not change his state of Illumination or the spiritual line in which he was working.

When you know, in your inner self, what your real destiny line is, it does not matter what happens on the outside; that is just the karma that comes and goes that you have to work through and neutralize. You always do your best, but you do not let it alter your spiritual destiny. That is the important thing to keep in mind. Once you have the Divine Feminine working through you, it will help you understand the processes of life correctly and get through the difficulties they create, while at the same time maintaining your orientation towards the Spiritual Reality. ✗

The Beatitudes

WHAT JESUS REALLY MEANT

CHAPTER 10

"*Only by establishing laws of conduct in human life can we re-establish the Divine Harmony within us. We may call these rules the Laws of the Higher Life.*"

The Laws of the Higher Life

There have been thousands of great Sages, such as Zoroaster, Hermes, Moses, the Manu, Buddha, Kṛṣṇa, Rāma, Lao Tzu, Confucius and Jesus Christ, and they have always been concerned with one problem: the basic disconnection of normal human life from the Divine Life, or the nonrecognition of the Divine Element in human existence.

This is why every one of the Teachers, without exception, drew up some rules of conduct. Moses gave the *Ten Commandments;* Jesus gave the Sermon on the Mount, or the *Beatitudes;* the Buddha established the Law as the *Wheel of Dharma.* Every one of them drew up a system of conduct because normal human beings are so disconnected from Reality that they need a guideline to reconnect themselves. Only by establishing laws of conduct in human life can we re-establish the Divine Harmony within us. We may call these rules the *Laws of Higher Life,* and they are always the same. They have to be the same, because they are based on the One Eternal Reality.

I will take an example from Jesus, called the *Beatitudes.* From there, we will establish what these basic laws of conduct are, and how we apply them in our lives.

The Origin of the Gospels

The original Teaching of Christianity was never written down in the early days. When Jesus talked, there were no tape recorders and there were no actual records of what happened. But some of the early disciples and followers made written recordings which were circulated as gospels. These gospels were what different people had heard, or what they thought they had heard, or their interpretation of what they had heard, second-hand, about the Teachings of Jesus and the Kingdom of God. Up until the fifth century there were several hundred of these gospels.

Then of course, the church became established as a materialistic kingdom. One of the Roman Emperors became converted to Christianity and he changed a religion which was purely spiritual into a dynamic, materialistic religion, a world empire. The Christian religion became a religion for conquering other nations, a power-trip for the Emperor, for the wealthy and the powerful.

Although there were many wonderful Teachings in Christianity, a lot of the Teaching was destroyed in the process because it conflicted with the materialistic drive of the emperor and the materialistic powers of the bishops who were controlling the church. They wanted to establish a solid, materialistic kingdom for themselves and to rule many nations. As a result, a lot of the fine Spiritual Teaching had to be destroyed because it was in total dissonance with what they were doing.

So the church selected four gospels as the Divine Inspiration, although originally there were many others. The other gospels were describing other realities, so they had to be destroyed. They threatened what the Emperor and the bishops were doing.

Furthermore, even the four gospels in the New Testament have been interfered with many times, because there are no known original manuscripts from the time of Jesus. Somebody may have written them down sixty, a hundred or two hundred years after the death of Christ, and these have been manipulated ever since, until some copies were "standardized" and said to be "the Gospel". So there were three hundred years or more for scholars to tamper with the written texts before they were finally even "standardized". So the accuracy of what you see there is very little.

Yet, even in those inaccurate transmissions which we have now as "the Gospels", the Truth shines through. You can definitely see that there was originally a Teaching. There is still something coming through very clearly. Jesus had a definite Teaching, even though it has been blurred, garbled and distorted beyond recognition by the materialistic elements in the church.

One of these Teachings is the Sermon on the Mount, the Beatitudes. Here, Jesus was giving the Laws of the Higher Life. He was doing a lot of public work, healing and everything else, and he was very tired. He went up a mountain and his disciples followed him. Then he sat down and began this discourse which we now know as the Sermon on the Mount, or the *Beatitudes*. You can see why this Teaching could be given only to his disciples, because the public couldn't understand it. The Beatitudes are essentially for the spiritual aspirants, the disciples, people who are on the Way or who want to experience the Spiritual Life.

The condition of society arises because the people are not responding to the Laws of the Higher Life. The Prophets had been giving the Jews the same Laws for about four thousand years before the birth of the Christ, but the Jews didn't listen to them. The Christians were given the same Laws by the Christ, but again, the Christians haven't listened for the last two thousand years. This is why the Christian world has always been in such a mess, and why it's not really Christian at all. "Christian" is only a name.

The Laws were given to the Jews, but they did not follow them. The Laws were given to the Christians, but they did not follow them. The Laws were given to the Arabs, but they did not follow them. This is the human pattern. The *Laws of the Higher Life,* the *Laws of Union* whereby the Oneness can be lived, are given by the Spiritual Hierarchy,[4] but people do not follow them.

---

4 *Spiritual Hierarchy:* Man's spiritual unfoldment is guided by the Planetary Hierarchy, the Great White Brotherhood, the Inner Government of the World, the Brotherhood of Light. It is also known as the Fifth Kingdom, the Kingdom of God, the Spiritual Kingdom, or the

The Beatitudes Today

I will first quote the teaching as it exists in the Bible today, and then we will go back to how the Teaching actually was, so that you have a more complete understanding of it. I'm going to explain to you, in very simple terms, what the Sermon on the Mount actually means, so that you can apply it to your own life, to your group life (which is more important), and then to the life of the world.

Following are the Beatitudes as they are found in the Bible today:

Blessed are the poor in spirit, for theirs is the kingdom of heaven.

Blessed are they that mourn, for they shall be comforted.

Blessed are the meek, for they shall inherit the earth.

Blessed are they which do hunger and thirst after righteousness, for they shall be filled.

Blessed are the merciful, for they shall obtain mercy.

Blessed are the pure in heart, for they shall see God.

Blessed are the peacemakers, for they shall be called the sons of God.

Blessed are they who are persecuted for righteousness' sake, for theirs is the kingdom of heaven.

Blessed are ye, when men shall revile you and persecute you, and say all manner of evil against you falsely, for my sake. Rejoice and be exceeding glad, for great is your reward in heaven. For so persecuted they the Prophets which were before you.

Matthew 5: 3–12

Christ-Hierarchy. It is the next human Hierarchy above the Human Hierarchy (the Fourth Kingdom). It is the Hierarchy of Saints, Masters, Yogīs and Teachers who have gone beyond the ordinary Man-type and are now evolving on the Causal, Buddhic and Nirvānic Planes. The Christ-Hierarchy also has Devas (Angelic Orders) working for them. This Hierarchy embraces the Nirvānic Realms, the Buddhic World and the formless Causal Worlds. It is from these realms that the Hierarchy sends down Avatāras, Divine Incarnations or Divine Messengers, to remind human beings of who they truly are, and to teach Mankind about the Kingdom of God. In Sanskrit, SANGHA or SATA-SANGHA.

Even if you leave the Beatitudes in this form, they still contain some sense of a guiding force. Yet, although Christians do read the Sermon on the Mount, it doesn't seem to mean anything because they don't understand some things about it. You can read it, but how do you relate it to your life? What does it actually mean? The problem with the gospels is that you can read them but not understand them, and then, of course, you don't apply them.

Remember that Jesus was giving this Teaching to his disciples. This is his inspiration of how his disciples should be living. Jesus was a realist; he always knew that the public wasn't necessarily going to follow these rules. But he gave these Laws to his own disciples to follow, so at least his disciples should have followed them in order to enter the Kingdom of God. Then, by transmission from his disciples, it was supposed to go out to the public.

Now we will go back to the original Teaching. I will take the Beatitudes one by one.

1. "Blessed are the poor in spirit, for theirs is the kingdom of heaven."

The first problem is the mistranslation: "kingdom of heaven." Originally, it was *Kingdom of God*. In the old Jewish language, there was no distinction between various layers of Reality, so the translators kept using the word "heaven". Heaven has nothing to do with the Kingdom of God; heaven is just a kind of happy state where you can go after death if you've done the right things. But Jesus wasn't talking about that blissful, imaginary, unreal heaven world. He was talking about the real Kingdom of God, that tremendous, dynamic Reality from where He descended, the *Kingdom of Light*.

Secondly, the teaching here is: "Blessed are the poor in spirit." In some modern translations it is made even worse. They say, "Happy are the *poor*, for theirs is the kingdom of heaven"! This is a totally wrong translation. It suggests that the kingdom of heaven is for the poor people—those who have no money, those who are poverty-stricken—but that's not what Jesus meant at all. He wasn't talking about poor people; he was talking about the *poor in Spirit*, or in modern terminology, the *humble* in Spirit. He meant those who have *surrendered* to the Spirit.

So you can see that the modern teaching is a complete departure from the Truth. This Law should read as follows:

Blessed are those who are humble in Spirit (who have surrendered themselves to the Spirit), for theirs is the Kingdom of God (the Divine Light).

In other words, if you want to reach the Nirvāṇic Light, the real Kingdom of God, the dynamic Kingdom of Reality from which Jesus descended, you have to become truly humble, or "poor in Spirit". You have to *surrender* yourself to the Spirit.

This is a completely different teaching than saying, "Happy are the poor." Most poor people are not really happy at all! This is just one example of how the New Testament has been distorted.

2. "Blessed are they that mourn, for they shall be comforted."

Here is another mistranslation. Again, it appears that those who are crying and unhappy shall be comforted. But, by the Law of Karma, if you're always unhappy you will remain unhappy, because you always generate the same karmic consequence.

This is not what Jesus meant, however. The actual Teaching he was giving was: "Blessed are those who are *yearning* or *restless* for Divine

Consciousness." He was talking about that ever-restless yearning for the Divine.

So, this Law should read as follows:

Blessed are they who are yearning for the Divine Consciousness, for they shall be comforted.

In other words, if you have that yearning for the Kingdom of God, then you shall receive It.

3. "Blessed are the meek, for they shall inherit the earth."

This is another example of the limitation of the Hebrew language. The word MALKUTH, or "Kingdom," has several meanings. One meaning is the physical Earth; another is the Universe itself; and another is the Kingdom of God. With such a variety of meanings, when the materialistic elements of the church became strong, they naturally twisted it to mean that if you are "meek", meaning gentle, then you will "inherit the Earth". But actually, you won't— everybody will trample you down!

In this context, Malkuth means the *Kingdom of God*, the Divine Reality. So the original Teaching is:

Blessed are those who are gentle, for they shall inherit the Kingdom of God.

4. "Blessed are they which do hunger and thirst after righteousness, for they shall be filled."

The real meaning here is: "Blessed are they who hunger and thirst for *right-mindedness*", not "righteousness" in the sense of "I am holier than thou".

You know how some Christians have this tremendous self-right-eousness. Everything is "of the devil" except what they happen to believe. What they believe in is the right thing, and everybody else goes to hell. That is not the kind of righteousness which is meant here!

Jesus was talking about *right-mindedness,* which is your mind being aligned with Reality, with the Truth Principle, established in the right-ness of things. So, what Jesus said was:

> **Blessed are they who hunger and thirst for right-mindedness, for they shall be fulfilled.**

This *right-mindedness* is also the Teaching of Kṛṣṇa, the Teaching of Buddha, the Teaching of Moses, and of all the great Prophets before.

5. **"Blessed are the merciful, for they shall obtain mercy."**

Well, that's pretty logical!

6. **"Blessed are the pure in heart, for they shall see God."**

This is also misunderstood. The Christians interpreted this sentence, "Blessed are the pure in heart," in terms of sexuality. They say that to be "pure in heart" you should have no sexual liaison with anyone; you become a celibate, a monk, a nun, or something like that.

But that is not the original meaning at all. It just means what it says: "the Pure in *Heart.*" To be "Pure in Heart" means that the Heart Chakra is pure, which simply means that there is no ego in your Heart. The ego acts as a kind of dross, impurity or film over the Heart and therefore you cannot see God. But if the Heart Chakra is open and the Love is flowing in a free way, without the ego blocking it, then in the Heart Chakra you can *see* God, in the most literal sense of the word!

Jesus was explaining to His disciples that if you drop the ego complex from the Heart, then you will actually see God. It has nothing to do with that insane "sexual purity" that the Christians have always had a mania about. They have always said that sex is dirty and impure, and therefore if you engage in sex, you are disconnected from the Divine Life. But that is another wrong slant of Truth. Here, there is no reference to sex at all; it just refers to the Heart Chakra. If the ego is not in your Heart, then you can see God. It is a very simple statement.

7. "Blessed are the peacemakers, for they shall be called the sons of God."

The whole Jewish background did not accept the Feminine Principle. God was always a father, ruler, king and lord, and God's children were always sons—never daughters! The Christians followed that male idea, as did the Muslims.

However, it is unlikely that Jesus meant that only males could attain these things. That is again a total slanting of the Teaching towards the Jewish male concept of the Divine. The correct sentence is:

Blessed are the peaceful, for they should be called the children of God.

RULES FOR DISCIPLESHIP

Seven qualities emerge from the seven Beatitudes we have discussed so far. These are the seven rules we have extracted from the seven Beatitudes, when rightly understood. They are qualities of the Laws of the Higher Life, the qualities of the disciple:

Humility.

Seeking God-Consciousness.

Gentleness.

Right-mindedness.

Mercy.

Purity of Heart.

Peacefulness.

Mercy means tolerance and Love, and *peacefulness* means nonviolence. So you have the quality of Love and the quality of nonviolence, and you will find that every Teacher, without exception, would teach exactly this: Love and nonviolence. You can go to the East or the West. You can go to Mahatma Gandhi, you can go to the Buddha, you can go to Moses, you can go to any Teacher, and they will teach you exactly that. When you sift this Teaching of Jesus from out of the Jewish context and from the misunderstandings and misinterpretation of the scholars, you find that same Universal Teaching about the qualities of a disciple.

These first seven rules are for you. They are your particular rules of conduct, and also the rules of conduct for a group. If a group applies these rules, then there will be total Harmony and Unity, and the group will experience the Divine Presence.

By extension, if the whole world could live like that, then the whole planet would be radically transformed. But you have to be realistic.

First you have to practise it yourself, and then you have to practise it as a group. This is why Jesus gave these rules first to his own disciples to practise, and then told them to teach them to the world. He knew exactly how the world would handle it.

There is an ancient saying: "Strong men are seldom moved by gentle motives."

These rules are "gentle motives". If you ask Mahatma Gandhi, the Buddha, Moses, or any other Teacher, they will be in total agreement with them. But strong men are seldom moved by gentle motives, and that is why the Kingdom of God has not been established on this planet. The "strong men" (meaning the rulers, the people in power, position, and authority) are not going to listen to this, so the world stays in a mess. It has nothing to do with God; it simply has to do with the strong men who are "seldom moved by gentle motives".

For a spiritual disciple, however, these rules have to be practised. You should practise these rules on a day-by-day basis: humility, seeking God-Consciousness, gentleness, right-mindedness, mercy or Love, purity of Heart and nonviolence. These are the basic, eternal Laws of Conduct. Keep them in mind as you go about your day; you will see that they will alter your own existence very rapidly.

If you can apply these Laws and practise this attitude in your life, then you are practising Discipleship. You are practising true Christianity, true Buddhism, true Hinduism. Whether you call yourself a Christian disciple or a disciple of the Truth, of God or of Reality, it is all the same. It is just the Eternal Law of Discipleship, the *Law of the Higher Life.*

The Christians misunderstand this. They believe that Jesus taught all these doctrines to everybody on the street, but that's another big mistake. It is just not so! Jesus taught His disciples away from the crowd. If you read the gospels very carefully, you will see that he did his healing and public ministry in the crowd, but then he would withdraw from the crowd with a small group of disciples and teach them about the Kingdom of God. It says in the gospel that he was tired and he went up to the mountains, and his disciples followed him. Then he sat down and taught this to his disciples—not the multitudes, not the millions of people, but his *disciples*.

This must be remembered: these are the rules for *Discipleship*. Ideally, of course, they are the rules for Humanity. Ideally, they should be applied by any group, organization, religion or community. They apply also to a family, a relationship between two people or a relationship between nations or tribes. Whether it's a larger or a smaller grouping, if we are to live together, these Laws have to be practised. Ideally, everybody should practise them, but the multitudes can never really do it, because they're just not in the right space to do it. At this stage you can only deal with the world by offering the Teaching. That is all you can do. You can't really go about and ask everybody to practise these principles.

The Rules of Discipleship can work only if people have *self-respect* and *self-responsibility*. It is only because people have no self-respect that they have no responsibility towards others, and it's because they have no sense of responsibility that they disregard the feelings and properties of others. Society's ills can be healed when everybody obeys the Rules of Discipleship, which is the Law which makes it possible for Mankind to again become the Children of God.

One Cannot Bend Karma

There have been many social systems invented by man—capitalism, communism, democracy, aristocracy, plutocracy, dreams and utopias, all kinds of systems—but none will work unless they are founded on the Eternal Law as exemplified by the seven Rules of Discipleship. These systems are not founded on right conduct, so naturally, they must fail! They simply won't work.

Out of these fundamental Laws of the Spirit have arisen the Jewish Talmudic system, the Arabic Koranic law and the Western Judiciary systems of statutes, laws and regulations. When the old Jewish Rabbis, the Church Fathers of Christianity and the Mullahs of the Muslim religion meddled with the Original Pure Law of the Spirit, they made it into a monstrous, devious system of so-called "justice". So the laws we have now are a far-removed reflection of the original Law. They have been tampered with, meddled with, added to, deviated from, and altered by human beings. It is a monstrous injustice to the original purity of the Law.

The cumbersome human legal system is full of loopholes and im-perfections. The law of the courts, as made by man, has no relevance to the Divine Law of Justice (Karma) which is undeviating, unbendable, unavoidable, and which cannot be cheated. The human law of every country is a made-up law which is always bent, twisted and turned around by the lawyers and the people.

But this Law is the Divine Law. It is the Law of Karma. One may cheat the human law, the system or the courts, but one cannot bend Karma. The supreme value of the Rules of Discipleship is to produce the right kind of karmas whereby the Kingdom of God may be regained. This is why Buddha, Rāma, Kṛṣṇa , Manu, Lao Tzu, Confucius, Moses, Zoroaster, Hermes Trismegistus, Mohammed, Socrates, Plato and many others all taught exactly the same Laws. It cannot be otherwise.

These rules are the rules for attaining the Kingdom of God. The Kingdom of God is in Mankind. Man, in his innermost nature, pos-sesses the particle of Light that is One with the Original Light, the

Kingdom of God, but Man has become shackled to his own ego and in bondage to the world. It is to redeem man from the world-consciousness and ego-domination that these Rules of Discipleship have been given. For behold, *the Kingdom of God is within you.*

So these are the rules of the Kingdom of God. The practising of these Rules of Discipleship will make you *allow* the Tao to enter.[5] To do that, you must prepare yourself, and the way of preparation is the practice of the seven Rules of Discipleship, which prepare you by wiping away your ego. If a person is driven by his ego and cannot surrender, then it is not possible for the Spirit to touch him. He remains locked up in his ego-consciousness all the time. That's why the Chinese say that you must *allow* the Tao to enter into you.

For instance, Purity of Heart (in the absolute sense) means pure egolessness, pure selflessness. Only a selfless Heart can be pure. It is just not possible to have a pure Heart which is full of ego. So the ego has to be completely removed before the Heart becomes pure.

Notice what Jesus said: "Blessed are the Pure in Heart, for they shall *see* God." He didn't say that they will learn about God, have symbols of God or be told about God; they shall actually *see* God! He refers to

---

5 TAO: The Chinese Sages have called Tao "the Great Absolute Ruler" and "the Heavenly-Master of Creation". Tao has also been described as the *Being* or *Essence* of all things, *the Source of active Power* within all things, the *Force* or *Energy* behind all forms. The Chinese word *Tao*, which predates Christianity by several centuries, is often translated as "the Logos" or "the Word", for Tao also means "to speak, to utter a sound, to express oneself by words". According to the ancient Chinese, Tao gave *order* to Primordial Matter, which then became Nature. Tao is transcendental and abstract, but, in its capacity as the subjective Power within Creation, it is God Immanent within the Universe *and* within Man.

Tao has also been translated as "the how of things, how things work, the meaning of things". For Tao *is* the ultimate meaning of all things, the *why and how* of all things, since beneath and within all objects is to be found Tao. (From *Heavens and Hells of the Mind* by Imre Vallyon.)

an actual experience! When the Heart is pure, when there is no ego functioning, the perception of the Divine becomes possible. So you see, these Laws have a very practical value.

The First Practice is Humility

You will find that these Laws lead one from the other. The first one to practise is humility, which is true surrender. From out of that comes the yearning for God-Consciousness. From that comes gentleness, which is non-aggressive, helpful behaviour. From that comes right-mindedness. From that comes mercy and tolerance. From that comes purity of Heart. And out of that comes true Peace.

So the first practice is humility. Realize that the ego is not everything, your mind is not everything, your fantastic learning is not everything, your wealth is not everything, your position in life is not everything. All of the things which you thought made you great are really of no importance. Then you begin to see yourself in a different light and you develop humility.

Once humility arises inside you, the yearning for God naturally arises; you begin yearning for the Infinite, the Absolute. Once that intense yearning begins to work in you, then naturally you develop gentleness, non-aggressive behaviour, helpfulness towards others. Then, as a natural consequence, you become in touch with the Truth Principle inside you, leading to right-mindedness. Then mercy, tolerance, charity and Love follow. When mercy, tolerance, charity and Love come to you, then purity of Heart, egolessness and self-forgetfulness come. Then, from out of the purity of Heart, Peace comes to you—real Inner Peace, that Peace which is of the Kingdom of God. It is a Peace coming from within, not from outer circumstances.

Remember that there are two kinds of peace. Jesus said, "I come to give you *my* Peace. The Peace that I give to you is not the peace of the world, but the Peace of the Kingdom of God."

Try to remember to apply these seven principles to your own life, and to your interaction with people. That is the way of the disciple! These rules apply always, whether you are a disciple of Jesus the Christ, the Buddha, Kṛṣṇa, Mohammed, Moses or any True Teacher. They are simply the *Law of Discipleship*.

THE EIGHTH AND NINTH BEATITUDES

The Principle of Opposition

Jesus added two other rules which are more difficult to comprehend. These two Beatitudes are rules for dealing with evil-minded people, people who use their minds in a destructive way against you when you become a disciple. This may be called the principle of the *opposition*.

The eighth Beatitude is a general statement. He says:

8. **"Blessed are those who are persecuted on account of their right-mindedness, for theirs is the Kingdom of God."**

Jesus is talking here about a general principle throughout the world. He is referring to all those Truth-seeking people who stand up for the Right and the True, the Beautiful and the Good, and whom others persecute. This was not necessarily just for his own disciples. He was stating the universal principle of opposition by Darkness wherever there is Light. If you are "right-minded" (if you are established in the Truth Principle), then you are bound to be persecuted.

In the last Beatitude, he was actually talking about his own disciples. He was extending the universal principle of opposition (the negative force) to the situation of his disciples:

"Blessed are you when they slander and persecute you, and falsely accuse you because of Me. Be glad, for in the Kingdom of God your reward is already great. For in the past they persecuted also the Prophets who went before you."

This principle is about His own disciples being persecuted by the world community. Jesus was talking in a very direct way about the Jewish reaction to what they were doing, because the Jews had already begun to persecute his disciples. He was talking about the evil mind whereby the Truth is rejected and whereby the person who teaches the Truth is persecuted. Jesus recognized that the opposition does exist, and that's why he included it in these Beatitudes.

"Me" refers to Jesus Christ in the historical setting in which Jesus spoke these words to his disciples, and it also refers universally to the Holy Spirit, the Divine Principle in Man. In other words:

Blessed is anyone who speaks for God, for the Truth, for the Divine Consciousness, and is persecuted by others for it.

So, the first seven Beatitudes have to do with you, while the last two are the recognition that there may be a repercussion from your environment to what you are doing. Jesus clearly recognized that. In the eighth and ninth Beatitudes, He expressed that recognition of a strong reaction when you represent the Spiritual Life. When people feel that you are in *right-mindedness*, which means that you live by the Truth Principle, they react to it.

The principle of opposition can be applied to a group as well. It is possible for somebody in a group to go wrong, and then that person will do the persecuting and make the false accusations which Jesus was describing. As you know, after this Sermon, one of his own disciples betrayed him. Judas then acted as the persecutor. One person from the group rose up and acted out that opposition. So Jesus explained the universal principle of opposition to the Kingdom of God by the mass mind, by the environment, as well as the possibility of persecution from within his own group.

He also mentioned: "They persecuted also the Prophets who went before you." This again refers to the Jews, because his own disciples were Jews, and the Jews had persecuted all of their Prophets. It also refers to a general principle in the world: people have always persecuted their Prophets. This is a tendency of the materialistic consciousness in the world. A good example was Jesus himself, who was also put to death.

So these last two Laws are simply about the repercussions from the world consciousness to the effort by the Spiritual Hierarchy to establish the Kingdom of God. They are about understanding the repercussions and just accepting that they are inevitable. As a general principle, *the Kingdom of God is difficult to establish here because people never give a chance to those who would be the messengers of the Kingdom of God.*

Abide By the Rules of Discipleship

The "evil mind", the "evil one", or symbolically the "devil", works through three things. Jesus actually mentions these three things:

Slander.

Persecution.

False accusation.

If you are on the side of Truth, Love, Goodness or Beauty, then evil-minded people will oppose you in these three ways: slander, persecution and false accusation. This has been repeated over and over again in history. The Jewish, Muslim and Christian religions are full of examples of this type of persecution of their Saints and of each other.

Jesus doesn't tell you how to deal with the evil-minded people. He just says that you are blessed when this happens to you, but he doesn't actually give a solution. He just acknowledges the fact that some people have evil minds and that they turn against you when you're trying to do good, when you're trying to do the Will of God, when you're obeying the Divine Principle within. He merely says that such things *are*.

Beforehand, however, He was describing the seven Laws of the

Disciple. So obviously, even when people are persecuting you, you still must abide by the seven Laws of Discipleship. In other words, you must not become like them. You must not render evil for evil, for instance, or hatred for hatred, or slander for slander, or persecution for persecution, or false accusation for false accusation. Simply abide by the Rules of Discipleship!

There is an old saying: "Where selfishness is fashionable, unselfishness is punished." This means that, in a society which is ruled by the ego-drives of selfishness, self-centredness, competitiveness and brutality, the gentle Laws of the Spirit seem to be out of place. Very often in the history of the Jewish, Christian and Muslim societies, the very people who practised these Rules of Discipleship were punished and persecuted by the evil-minded.

Jesus commented on this terrible situation. He said that a true disciple has no choice but to obey these rules. "For what does it profit a man, if by ego-drives he gains the whole world, but suffers the loss of his Soul?" ⋠

Silence

CHAPTER 11

"*In Silence, when all thoughts have been put to rest,
the Mind-field opens up its treasures for viewing and
one begins to observe an Immense Reality.*"

There is a Place where there is no birth and no death, where there is no time for questioning by the mind. It is the *State of Silence*.

The Sufi Masters

From the Unfathomable *Original-Silence*, there appeared a great Power, the Mind of the Universe, which manages all things, which is a male, CHOCKMAH; and another Power, a great Intelligence, which is female, which is the producer of all things, which is called BINAH, the Mother of all things.

The Gnostics

According to the very early Gnostics (the Illumined Christians), Silence is the Primordial Root of all things. It is the Fountainhead of Reality. Out of That appears the Universal Mind, which is like the manager of things, and the great Creative Intelligence, the producer of all things, which is the female aspect, the *Mother*.

Krishnamurti also speaks of Silence:

Meditation is the emptying of the content of the mind, where thought comes to an end, in *Silence*. Meditation is the attention, or Choiceless Awareness, in which there is no registering. Out of that comes *Silence*, because thinking has come to an end. When there is Silence, there is an Immense *Timeless-Space*, which is the *Eternal*, the *Sacred*.

This is Krishnamurti's experience. He entered that Silence and discovered Timeless-Space, which is the Eternal and the Sacred. This is very much the same as the *Original-Silence* of the Gnostics, out of which everything came forth.

In Sūfism, this condition is called *Murāqabah*, or "the way of no fixed concentration" or "Choiceless Awareness".

I am quoting many sources so that each will lead you to a better understanding of the subject. Now I shall quote from Buddhism:

Silence is a meditation, devoid of mental concentration, a dissolution of mental activities, there being no such thing as action (KARMA) or a performer of the action (the AHAṀKĀRA, the ego).

In Tibetan Buddhism, this teaching on Silence is called the *Supreme Way of Bon.* This State of Silence is described as:

Just relax yourself spontaneously in the Mind-Essence Itself, in the Mind's natural, original condition. This is the condition of the Primeval Buddhahood, the essence of Knowledge in the natural state, which is an Absolute Purity and an unconditioned Void, or Emptiness of forms. This condition is known as the *Great,* the *Unmoved,* and has no first-existing origin, nor an intermediate way or progressive stages, nor a final attainable end.

What is being described is a State of Silence which is not simply "not talking," or not making any sound; it is a very profound condition having to do with *Original Reality.* All of these Teachings describe Silence in terms of the Original Reality, which we attain by a certain cessation of mental movements. This Silence comes about by emptying the mind of all contents. The Christians of the Middle Ages used to call it *Contemplation.*

Contemplation, or the State of Silence, requires a serene mind, empty of thoughts, and a calm daily life. This is why it was very suitable during the Middle and Dark Ages and the early period of the Christian era. The pace of life was very slow in those days—especially for some monks and nuns of the Church—so they could spend lots of time in what they called *Contemplation,* or entering into that Silence of no mind-action. That's why the last two thousand years have produced so many Christian mystics; they arrived at that state by Contemplation.

This State of Contemplation, or Silence, is not emptiness in a negative sense. It is not a laziness nor an idleness of the mind. This has to be understood. It is a very high state of *mental alertness*—what in the East has been called "Choiceless Awareness". This mental alertness, or Choiceless Awareness, is a state of *noncritical mind* which accepts the duality of *what is*, without taking sides. In the State of that Silent Mind, you just see things as they are. As soon as you take sides, your Silence disappears. You will know this from experience.

The State of Silence is an Inner Stillness that comes from the Soul. The outer faculties (the body, mind, ego and emotions) merely conform to that Inner Stillness. There is a Union of all the various parts of the human being—what, in India, is called Yoga. You feel in this Silence a completeness, wholeness, togetherness and centring within yourself.

When the Divine Silence is established within you, you become aware of a Formless World, a spaceless, timeless dimension where the Will of God operates alone. It is a Realm of Bliss, Freedom and Existence. It is like a Vast Inner Space. The Buddhists call this condition *Mahashunyata* (MAHĀŚŪNYATĀ)—the Great Emptiness, the Great Inner Space. In this Great Silence, or Emptiness of Forms, you perceive the Root-Cause of all things, as is described by the Taoist Sage Lao Tzu:

> Touch the Ultimate Emptiness, hold yourself steady and still, and you will see that all things work together.
>
> For in this Silence, I have watched all things reverting, being born, then flourishing, and ultimately returning to the Root of all things—the Tao, the Emptiness, the Silence.
>
> This I say is the Silence, a return to one's own Roots, a return to the Will of God, which is *Permanency*. The experience of this Permanency I call *Enlightenment*, and not to know it is Spiritual blindness, which works much evil.
>
> When you know from experience this Inner Silence, which Eternally is always the Same, you have Dignity. This Dignity produces *right-mindedness*, and right-mindedness is royal, and this kingliness is *Divinity*, and this Divinity of Man is the *Way*, which is final.

The Zen Master, Huang Po, described this Silence as follows:

> This *Primordial Mind* we are speaking of is not a mind of ordinary, conceptual thinking. It is totally *formless* and *empty*, like a *void*. In it you realize that all the Buddhas and all the sentient beings, including yourselves, are not different at all. If only you could bring yourself to become Still and stop your normal thinking patterns, then you would have accomplished everything.
>
> If you who consider yourselves disciples of the Spiritual Path cannot still your minds and empty the mind of discursive thought-processes, then even if you strive for discipleship for a million aeons, you will never accomplish Enlightenment.

In the beginning, a group of people will feel very shy and awkward being together in silence. They fidget; they don't know what to do with themselves; they feel very self-conscious. You may have experienced this. In previous Retreats we could only have a certain amount of silence because people couldn't bear to be together in silence for too long. This individual and group barrier to silence has to be overcome before the spontaneous and natural Silence of Contemplation can begin.

In the Natural Silence of Contemplation, people are *spontaneous* in their togetherness and Silence. That means that when we walk in Silence, for instance, nobody says anything, yet we are still together. We don't feel isolated just because nobody has said anything to us for the last ten minutes. That feeling of togetherness is unbroken.

In normal life, people feel left out if somebody doesn't talk to them every five minutes. But when you have Silence, the group doesn't feel the need to talk. They "speak by Silences". Silence is a speech in itself. This also refers to the mystics and the great Teachers. They "speak by Silences". Silence is a form of radiation. They understand one another without words.

A deeper Silence develops when, naturally and spontaneously, even thoughts fall away, and the mind is completely emptied of images, ideas, thoughts and forms.

The third stage of Silence is when this is so permanent that it remains with you under all conditions—while you're talking, thinking, walking, eating, living, working, and living an ordinary life. If the Silence remains with you under all conditions, then you have attained the true *State of Silence*.

The Tibetan Book of the Great Liberation describes this Silence as follows:

> This Silence is the *true State of Mind*. And the Mind in this condition is naked, empty, immaculate, not made up of anything, like a great Empty Space. The Mind in this Silence is empty, clear, without perceiving Duality of Opposites, transparent, eternal, simple, unified, and quality-less.

Every mystical writer who has experienced this condition describes it in practically the same terms. It is a State of Unity. It is the State of the Mind Itself, the *Mind-Essence*. It is empty, like a void or a space. The description is the same everywhere.

From what we have illustrated to you, one comes to the conclusion that Silence is the Primary Condition of the Mind—not only of your own mind, but also of the Mind of the Universe. Because, what is true for you is true also for the Cosmos, and what is true for the Cosmos is also true for you.

Your own primary Mind-Condition is Silence, and the primary Condition of the Mind of the Universe, the *Cosmic Mind*, is also Silence. This is why both ancient and modern authors who attained Inner Silence, that State of Union, describe the Original Divine Mind, or Source, as *Silent*. They perceived that same Silence in the Cosmos as they perceived within themselves.

Only when the mind is tranquil can one become aware of the Whole Mind, the Totality of Mind. In Silence, when all thoughts have been put to rest, the Mind-Field opens up its treasures for viewing and one begins to observe an Immense Reality. In the complete Silence and Stillness of the Soul, you discover the creativity of the mind, and the illusions, mistakes and aberrations that you call your "life". When you *see* these mistakes, illusions and aberrations created by your mind, they will no longer have any hold on you. If you discover a fault and see it clearly, you will be free from that fault. In the recognition of that Truth, the Karma is immediately wiped out. You discover something about yourself, and that Truth will make you free. This is what Jesus meant when he said: *"The Truth shall make you Free"* (John 8: 32).

This is the tremendous value of Silence. Silence is an amazingly healing, recreating, holistic, integrating process. It neutralizes your tensions, aggressions, fears, worries, depressions and all negative qualities.

True Silence and Tranquillity leads to meditation in a spontaneous way. It is transforming in quality. By remaining in Silence, one enters into deeper and deeper stages of meditation and Unity with the Godhead, the Divine Mind. In Silence, we perceive the *Infinite* and experience the *Eternal*.

Silence is a state of "Choiceless-Awareness", or *no concentration at any point*. There are meditational processes which are concentrations at a point—whether it's a mantra, an image, a sign, a symbol or an object—but this practice is *no fixed concentration at any point*. It is simply *Awareness*. In this condition, the Mind is the Witness to everything that takes place, within and without, but it is not disturbed by any phenomena—neither by the world nor by the thoughts in the mind.

Silence is the regaining of one's Spiritual Roots, the *Essence* within you. When the Silence is very deep, on the level of the Cosmic Mind, you become what the Hindu Yogīs call the *Witness*. You become the Witness of phenomena. If you react to phenomena, however, then you have moved away from the Original Silence. If you are aware of the Silence behind your daily life but are still agitated by the phenomenon of living, then your Silence is not complete. It is not penetrating to the roots. You are still in the field of action, touching upon the Field of Silence. Once you merge completely into the Silent Field, then you become a Witness to your own life process, yet you are not disturbed within by that life process.

The Lord Buddha taught a similar practice:

> Like a broken gong, be silent, be still. This Silence, this Stillness, is Nirvāṇa, where there is no more striving.

When you enter the profound Silence of the Cosmic Mind, that is Nirvāṇa. But notice that there is "no more striving" in it, no more aggression. Everything takes place, but inside you are free from that striving, that aggression of living.

You can still be naturally active, however. It is only at the beginning stages that you separate action from Silence. When you are completely merged into Silence, you can still be active; you can still do things; you can think, feel and act, yet nothing moves that integrity of the Inner Silence.

This is the Zen meaning of: "Sitting quietly doing nothing". This is a silent, choiceless observation of all events, all thoughts, all feelings, without attempting to interfere with what actually is, without allowing the ego to dominate a situation. In this State of the Silence of the Mind, there is no repression and no condemnation, neither self-praise nor self-criticism. You do not repress facts, truths or situations. There is just the *Witness*.

The Mind dwells in the Stillness, the ego dies in the Stillness, and the Light shines forth from the Higher Self. When the mind becomes still, the ego feels that it dies, and at that moment the Light shines forth from the Self.

The Lord Buddha said:

> Do not complain about your life. Do not cry. Do not be angry. Do not pray for deliverance. Do not criticize. Be *Silent*, and you will open your inner eyes and see.
>
> For the Truth is all about you, like a great Silent Space, and you will discover it if you take the bandage from the eyes of your mind.
>
> This Silence, this Stillness, this Truth is so wonderful. It is so far beyond anything that the minds of men have dreamed of. And it lasts forever.

This Silence has also been described in *The Tibetan Book of The Great Liberation*:

> All hail to this One Mind, that embraces the whole of Saṁsāra and the whole of Nirvāṇa, that eternally is as it is, and yet remains unknown to so many. It is always clear and ever-existing. It is not visible to the physical eyes, yet it is the Radiant and Unobscured *Silence*. It is not recognized by the worldly-minded.

From these many quotations from the East and West, you can see that Silence is more than people think it is. It is infinitely more powerful in potential. Initially, it may appear to be a very simple practice—simply sitting still and doing nothing, or walking in the woods and being quiet, or being quiet with another person—but the end results are tremendous. It leads you to the Highest Realization. You have the testimony of all of those Great Beings who practised Silence.

Silence begins with the quietening of the thoughts and ends with the recognition of the *Infinite Mind*. So what may appear to be a simple practice of no-thinking ends up as a Cosmic Revelation.

There is a very profound statement from the great School of Christian Mysticism, from the experience of Silence:

They Speak by Silences.

This saying has several profound meanings. An extension of this statement is: "They speak by Silences, but we must be ready to hear."

Who could "They" possibly be? Increasingly, as you practise Silence, you will come to know what it means. You will become increasingly aware of "They".

They who Speak by Silences are actually certain types of Beings. There is a whole Hierarchy of Superhuman beings who have attained the Nirvāṇic Consciousness: the Nirmāṇakāyas, the Buddhas, and all the great Mystics and Saints of all times, human and nonhuman. There is an Eternal Communion, which comes about through the Power of *Silence.* When you enter the world of Silence, then you know that they communicate with one another by pulsations of Silence.

This is how you can become Enlightened; this is how you also can have Divine Revelation and Divine Wisdom; this is how you can be taught by truly Higher Beings—by *Silence.*

This is the inner meaning of *They Speak by Silences.* As the mystic moves into deeper strata of Silence he begins to hear the messages of these Divine Illumined Beings. These are not messages by words; they are by the process of *Revelation.* It is a Silent Knowing, an Intuitive Knowing, a Direct Revelation. Sometimes it can be visionary, but it could be just an intuitive perception of something, or a silent transmission.

In this way, you can hear the great Symphony of Minds in the Cosmos, the Divine Minds of all Beings speaking to you in the Silence. They speak by pulsations of Silence. When something appears in your mind, it's just like a silent music handed over to you in an instant, and already they have conveyed something to you.

So the statement *They Speak by Silences* refers to two things. As we become mystics, we communicate increasingly by Silence. A lot of *this* message is being communicated by Silence. A lot of the Inner Teaching of the Divine Mysteries is communicated by Silence. Even on the level of the beginner mystics—human beings who are on the Path—the silent communication is already being formed, and the essential communication is done through the pause between words or the pause between thoughts.

Then, as we practise Silence, we become increasingly identified with the Higher Beings who function in Higher Spheres and whose communication is by rhythmic pulsations of Silence.

PRACTISING SILENCE

Just enter into Silence. Remember, this is a condition of Natural Stillness which arises from no-thinking. It is a *natural* way of not thinking. It is not a concentration, but a no-concentration. There is no specific object to concentrate on; it is a natural, attentive *Awareness* of all things inside and outside you.

In most forms of Yoga you have a specific object to concentrate on. But this way, *the Way of Silence,* is a condition of Choiceless Awareness, in Profound Stillness. You are wide awake, but your mind is not grasping this thought or that thought, this condition or that condition. You are not grasping things with your mind and ego. Just hear the Silence and become the Silence.

You don't have to split yourself. You can still perform your normal actions and remain silent. You don't have to sit rigidly in one place. You can be active, you can think, feel and do things normally, but at the same time abide in that State of Silence within.

In this way, something happens in your life which is radically different. You become increasingly Unified with the All-Mind, the Divine Mind, the Presence of God. Whatever you do, the Presence of God shines through that action. This is the Practice of Silence.

Stand Before your Lord and Maker in Awe and Silence

This is a Jewish practice called *Selah,* or Silence. You realize the Presence of God and remain silent. It doesn't matter where you stand; you may be standing in your kitchen or you may be standing outside in Nature. Just remain completely silent, with the sensation of awe.

Awe means that you realize that the Divine is present in all things visible and invisible. It gives you a tremendous feeling of the Presence of God, which also silences your mind. The more awe you feel, the more silent your mind becomes, and the more silent your mind becomes, the greater the feeling of the Presence of God.

Waiting Upon the Lord in Silence

A Christian practice is to "Wait upon the Lord in Silence" or "Listen to the footsteps of the Lord." It has been compared to what is called the *sentry*, when you imagine yourself to be like a watchman or a sentry and wait and listen in silence and expectation for the footsteps of the Lord.

In Christian understanding, the State of Silence can come about only by True Surrender to the Divine Will—not the will of the ego, but deeper, in the Silence of the Self, the Holy Spirit, the Christ within.

Keeping Silence

There is a Hindu Yoga practice called *Mauna*, "Keeping Silence". In this practice, you try to keep that State of Silence all day long. This is more difficult. The Yoga practices are okay if you are living by yourself in a cave—then it's easier to practise Silence—but it's different when you are living in a community. In this practice, you don't talk and you don't think. Your mind does not move at all. It is very effective but it's not very suitable if you are in a community. You can do it at certain times, however. You can choose a time during the day when you practise *Mauna*, or "Keeping Silence".

The Recognition of Divine Unity

This Sufi practice is as follows:

> When you stand in Silence before Creation, you behold the Face of God.

To understand this, you must first understand the Sufi saying:

> The Resplendent Silence, Allah, is One. Allah alone Is.

This means that Creation, or what you behold before your eyes, is God's manifestation or emanation from His own Light-Substance or Eternal Splendour. This is the Oneness of Creation and Allah. This is the Divine Unity, or *Tawhīd*.

God is not separate from what you behold with your physical eyes. That is the Oneness of all things, the Divine Unity, the *Tawhīd*. Even while you look at the Sun, the Moon, the stars, the trees, the oceans and the mountains, you are actually beholding "the Face of God".

In this Sufi practice, if you become Still and look at Creation, you recognize that Allah is before you. You begin to see the Face of God, the Form of God. As your Silence deepens, you immediately begin to perceive the Light, the Shining Intelligence behind the form of God. That is *Allah*, the *Resplendent Silence*.

Waiting for the Light of Allah

A Muslim practice is to stand in Silence at midnight and wait for the Light of Allah. Allah is *God*, the *Light beyond compare*, the *Eternally Effulgent One*, the *Resplendent Silence*. You practise this for about an hour at midnight. You would usually have your hands together in a prayer attitude and you simply wait for the Light of Allah to appear. This is a most beautiful practice.

COMMUNICATING BY SILENCE

If two human beings on this level of evolution want to speak by *Silence*, it's not enough for them not to *say* anything; they must not *think* anything either. When you walk with a person or sit next to a person, you must not direct a whole stream of mental activity to that person. That's not communicating by Silence.

If two human beings really communicate in Silence, there is no need for talking, no need for thinking. You can just walk through the woods without a word being said, without a thought being thought, yet there is an amazing communication taking place in that Silence.

This is the meaning of the Zen "mind-to-mind" transmission. When you have a mind-to-mind transmission, the Teacher just sits. The Teacher does not think, the Teacher does not speak, yet a silent radiation goes out from the Teacher. This is *Communication by Silence.*

You can do that with others too. Simply be together in the same space; there's nothing more that needs to be done.

It's amazing how many teachings or exchanges can take place between two people in this way. You don't even need to think about anything or say anything. Simply be together in Silence. That's all that needs to happen.

Many people are shy just to be together in Silence. They don't know what to do, so they become agitated and start fidgeting and they start thinking rapidly and furiously. They can't just be in total Silence without doing anything or accepting the other person just as they are. There always has to be some kind of furious physical-mental activity. But if people stop fidgeting and drop the mental activity, then it doesn't matter. You can sit next to each other, walk next to each other, work together in the kitchen or do anything together, and you don't have to say anything. You discover that you can coexist without having to say anything to a person.

Now that is quite a revelation! In the normal world we think that communication is endless talking, mental telepathy, or projecting thoughts to a person; but we discover that just being in Silence is actually a more powerful communication.

In the beginning it feels strange. Many people don't like it; they feel that they have to say something or do something. With a bit of practice, however, you can just be together for hours without saying anything at all, having no mental concepts or thoughts about anything. In this way, you will develop an amazing sense of togetherness and Unity.

LISTEN TO SILENCE: SILENCE IS ETERNITY

Listen to Silence. Silence is Eternity.
Unlearn all things. Simple Unity is the best.
The ego needs do nothing.
Doing nothing, the One Self does everything.

The stuff of the Universe, out of which all things are made, is Mind-Stuff. It is the One Mind.

At no time do the body, mind and ego exist as separate entities. The feeling of separation arises with the sense of *time*. The body is born, grows old and dies. This appears to be a passage through time. Similarly, the mind appears to go through changes over the years, which also involves time. The ego has a longer duration, involving thousands of lives, but it also is subject to what is called "time".

Time is a relative sensation of the perception of events as is registered by the body-mind-ego complex, the "personality". Time depends on a past, present and future on a horizontal line.

But the Essential Self within you is in a Timeless Condition and a Limitless Space. Since the Essential Self within you is in a Timeless Condition, then, in the process of Enlightenment or Union with God, there is no need for you to consider time. Eternity is *now!* That which you seek, you already are.

Do not have a longing to become a future Buddha. Do not think that you will reach Enlightenment in the future. *The ego needs do nothing. Doing nothing, the One Self does everything!*

To become Enlightened, to be "saved", to attain the goal of Yoga, to attain Union with God or At-One-Ment are goals of the ego. The ego says, "If I practise this and that, I will be able to attain Enlightenment in the future." But, *the ego needs do nothing. Doing nothing, the One Self does everything.*

Unlearn all things. Abiding in a Simple Unity is the best. It is a simple surrender. True surrendering is the non-action of the ego.

We are compounded out of the Eternal Mind. Stillness is the silencing of all thoughts, when the Light of Eternity is made manifest. In this Stillness is the unlearning of all things. This is simple Unity. It is the best. In Silence is the door to Eternity. For *the ego needs do nothing. Doing nothing, the Self does everything.*

This is a very profound Enlightenment for you. Meditate on this Stillness. Previously, you listened for sound; in this practice, you listen to *Silence.*

It is because you have learned too much that you cannot perceive the Simple Reality. The mind has become over-complicated, and the more complex the mind is, the less chance you have of perceiving the Essential Reality. Stillness is the unlearning of all things. By putting your mind back into the Stillness, all this complexity of the mind will disappear. Your mental activities are merely superfluous activities of the mind; as you abide more and more in Stillness, you will see how thoughts become quiet and disappear. When the thoughts disappear, the Original Mind appears, and then you perceive the Essential Unity of all things. That is why I say that simple Unity is the best.

Meditate on this simple Union and Stillness. By abiding in the Stillness, align yourself to unlearn everything that you ever learned. Remember, *the ego needs do nothing. Doing nothing, the Self does everything.* This is the Realization which comes out of the Stillness.

This practice is the complementary form of *The Listening Attitude.* In the practice of The Listening Attitude, we were listening for sound: inner sounds, outer sounds, nature sounds, all kinds of sounds. In this practice, you listen for *Silence*. It will completely shift your attention. Very soon you will realize that *Silence is Eternity.*

Before you go to sleep, or whenever you have a moment, listen to the Silence. Don't think that there is nothing to be heard. *Listen to Silence. Silence is Eternity.* You don't listen for sounds; you listen for *Silence.* Even when you go out into Nature, you don't listen to the sounds of Nature; you listen to Silence.

At the same time, bear in mind that *the ego needs do nothing. Doing nothing, the Self does everything.* This means that you need not seek Enlightenment. The less you seek it, the quicker you get there. Just put yourself in the State of Silence, and everything happens. The Self does everything. ✗

Daily Meditations

CHAPTER 12

Wherein the reader is offered an ongoing system of meditation, inspired by subtle and poetic truths from on High, to be read, reflected upon, and realized.

MEDITATION INSTRUCTIONS

The following pages contain a system of meditation. These Mantras are *Words-of-Power-by-Thought*. Some Mantras work by the power of sound-vibrations, but these work by the power of *thought*. Thought has great power to rule, to guide, to transform.

Each of these "thoughts" in the following pages come from an interior Realization, a Revelation born in Cosmic Consciousness. They are not just ordinary thoughts, popping into the mind when it is idle; they are things seen from the point of view of *Higher Consciousness*. Do not mistake them for some cosy, nice, positive thoughts that will hopefully change you. They are statements of *fact* about you which I have received from the state of Higher Consciousness. Perhaps, at this stage of your practice, you may not recognize yourself in such a way, but these Words of Power will reveal to you your true nature.

This form of meditation is Raja Yoga, the Yoga of the Mind, using Mantra. It should be practised internally, in formal meditation, as well as in all circumstances of your life.

The Inner Practice

Repeat the Words of Power aloud several times to yourself, very slowly.

e.g. *"The Spirit of Infinite Power is within me."*

Repeat the Words of Power *inwardly,* silently in your mind, very slowly. Dwell on the meaning of the Mantra. Consider all of its implications in your life and how this truth changes your whole perception of life. Can you think it through, what it really means, that *the Spirit of Infinite Power is within you?* What amazing possibilities does it reveal to you? What amazing changes can it bring into your life?

Break the Mantra down and reflect on the parts.

e.g. *"The Spirit of Infinite Power... ...is within me."*

Then reduce the Mantra to the essential truth. Go into it in great detail in your mind.

e.g. *"The Spirit of Infinite Power."*

Then reduce the words further still, to an essential word.

e.g. *"The Spirit."*

By this time, if you have practised correctly, your mind will have stopped. You will have entered the great Silence of *Insight,* of *Realization,* of *Revelation.*

The Outer Practice

Hold the Mantra in your mind all day long. Dwell on each sentence over and over again. Keep it in your mind always, hour after hour, day after day, under all circumstances. Act as if it were true—which, in fact, it is! As you act from that plateau of understanding, suddenly it will become true for you as an actual Reality. These Mantras are the You speaking to the you. Each sentence is a treasure-house.

It is recommended that you dwell on each Mantra for at least two days. Or if you wish, you may work with each Mantra for several days or weeks until your Realization of it is complete, full, perfect.

There is no hurry in this practice. You cannot hurry your realization process. You have to grow into it. You have to "grow up" spiritually.

If you understand what I have said above and practise faithfully, you shall walk with the Gods and the Power of God shall rest upon you!

Do not think that this is a beginner's form of meditation. In fact, it is very advanced! It is a mental Yoga; your focus is in the mind. But if you do it well, you shall converse with your Soul.

DAILY MEDITATIONS

1

The Spirit of Infinite Power is within me. My essence is
God's very own Essence. My life is hid in God's Life.

2

Identification with the body is the bondage of Mankind.
I am greater than my bodily powers and abilities. I
am greater than all limitations imposed upon me by
birth, heredity, environment and circumstances.

3

My True Nature is Limitless Life, Absolute Freedom and
Fullness of Power. I dwell upon the mountain peaks
of Realization and the summit of Achievement.

4

I descend into the Valley of Life with full confidence
in my own God-given powers, knowing that all
problems, difficulties and pains that life presents to
me will be overcome and surmounted by the Spirit
of Infinite Power, of which I am an open channel.

5

Nothing can prevent me from becoming
what I want to be. Nothing can stop me from
attaining my Goal. The Force is with me.

6

I think in new Categories. I reach out for new
Horizons. I open myself up to the Limitless Life. I
break through all limitations. Limitless opportunity is
mine. I have the potential for unlimited growth.

7

I am cheerful, happy and bright. I am confident and well,
for the Power that energizes the Suns and the Stars of the
Universe flows through me also. My life is a total success.

8

I am One with the Cosmic Intelligence that
plans all Creation. I am an instrument of the
Higher Self, unfolding the Cosmic Plan.

9

I am One with the Joys, the Successes and the Victories
of the Superconscious Intelligence. My life is full of
miracles. The Universal Spirit works through me.

10

I am an open channel for the Miracle of God's
Power. I participate daily in God's Ever-New
Joy. My life is a Miracle of His Expression.

11

I and my Father are One. There is only One Being, One Will, One Mind. All that exists and all that I am is an expression of the One Will. I am One with the Eternal Being now, and my Life is a Radiance of Its Presence.

12

I am not my thoughts. I am not my actions, feelings and desires. I am something that is above thought, feeling and action.

13

I am the Eternal Wanderer in the Valley of Time. I am the Eternal Sojourner upon the High Ways of Life. I am a Flame of Livingness, a Spark of Him who ever was and always shall be.

14

There never was a time when I was not. There never shall be a time when I shall cease to be. For the Self and I are One, for all Eternity.

15

I direct my mind positively toward wholesome goals and positive expressions. I make my feelings positive also. I think only of Happiness, Well-Being and Success. Happiness, Well-Being and Success will come to me as surely as the Sun rises and sets.

16

I let the Truth of my Being shine in my life, and Life will shine with me and for me, like the Splendour of a thousand Suns.

17

My physical body is not separate from the Sea of the Universal Mind. The Soul of the World builds my body to be an instrument of my Higher Self. The Universal Subconscious Mind controls all my bodily processes. I am radiating Love, Health and Happiness.

18

All beings are in continuous telepathic rapport through the interconnecting links of the Universal Mind. My subconscious mind transmits images of Health, Love and Happiness to all people around me.

19

The Primordial Virgin Substance unites me with the One Life. I share my life with all Creation through the interwoven fabric of the Universal Subconscious Mind.

20

All things that I experience with my five senses are, in reality, pictures or images, thoughtforms held in the Ocean of Universal Mind.

21

By the powers of my subconscious mind, I attract perfect
Peace and Wisdom, Happiness and Serenity, Love and Health.

22

I am telepathically attuned to all Life. My subconscious
mind is linked to the Universal Mind, and through the
Universal Mind I am linked even to the most distant stars.

23

I am serene and peaceful, poised, confident, patient, enduring
and steady, because my life is One with the Universal Life,
and my substance is One with the Cosmic Essence.

24

All Knowledge is Eternal and is available to Mental
Sympathy. My mind is One with the Infinite Mind. I
draw upon the Wisdom of the Mind of Light. God's
Peace is with me now. Peace and Wisdom are mine.

25

My subconscious mind has the scroll of memory
reaching back to the beginnings of time. I erase all
negative patterns that held me back from total Love,
Happiness and Fulfilment. I live in Peace and Serenity.

26

All my psychic powers are unfolding safely in me under
the conscious guidance of my Higher Self. I am passive
and receptive to the Fluidic Ocean of the psychic
world. I am consciously existent in the Astral World.

27

The associative powers of my subconsciousness are
controlled by the skilful self-direction of my conscious mind.
Through self-conscious direction of the astral substance I
experience Superconscious Awareness and Higher Wisdom.

28

I free my subconscious mind from the lower
levels of thought of the mass-mind, and receive
telepathically the Wisdom of the Higher Self.

29

I utilize the powers of the Astral Sea but do not become
submerged by it. Through my subconscious mind I am united
to all Wisdom and my life reflects the Peace of the Infinite.

30

I am opening myself up to the Divine Will. I am a
channel for the Spiritual Energies of the Higher Self. I
am directing the Superior Forces of the Real World.

31

I have the ability, skill and power to fulfil all of my heart's desires. I am confident and successful because I am a channel for Omnipotent Forces to accomplish all my plans.

32

My life is One with the Universal Life, and the Universal Forces flow through me. I am being helped by the Directive Power of the Superconscious Mind.

33

I am attentive and alert to all opportunities. I control all my forces and focus them on the successful outcome of my desires. I concentrate my energies on my goal, and attain.

34

The Limitless Power of the Infinite attunes my life to the flow of Superior Forces. I have initiative and skill to become what I wish to be. The Master Power works through me right now.

35

I penetrate into the real meaning of every situation in my life and I arrange my circumstances according to the Divine Will. I and my Father are One.

36

What I experience depends on what I focus my attention upon. By paying attention to a thought or an idea, I bring it about. What I think about shapes my Destiny.

37

My subconscious mind is the source of all the patterns which become my life's experiences, and my subconscious mind is under the direction of my will. My will is attuned to the Divine Will.

38

I am self-confident and possess an indomitable Will, for the Power of the Eternal works through me. I ask my Father what I will, and from the inexhaustible supply of Limitless Substance He grants all my requests.

39

The Sun of Life warms me. The True Spiritual Sun regenerates me. I surrender my life to the guidance of the Blazing Sun of Spirituality.

40

I have perfect confidence and faith in Life because the Inexhaustible Energy of the Sun courses through my veins. The Golden Radiance of the Sun binds me to my Beloved.

41

I am Loved and I Love, and the waves of Love, warmth
and security fill me through and through.

42

I am permeated with the Light of Love, the Sunshine of
Happiness and the Radiance of Accomplishment. Through
my personality I am radiating the Sun of Eternal Creativity.

43

I Love Life, I Love God, I Love Humanity. I am a
Ray of the Eternal Self shining endlessly.

44

I am born anew each day. I face each day with joyous
anticipation, like a child. I forget the limitations of
the past and press on with the new opportunities
of the present. My future is Infinitely Bright.

45

I take refuge at the Shield of Love of the Divine Mother,
who protects and sustains me. The Cosmic Mother
protects me. The Light of Her Presence enfolds me.

46

My personal world is changing as I implant new
images of Love and Well-Being, Prosperity and
Success, into the field of my subconsciousness.

47

The Divine Mother builds me a new future according
to my Heart's desire. O Cosmic Mother, let me awaken
now to the full knowledge of my own Divinity! Let me
awaken to the knowledge of my own Creative Powers!

48

I am One with the Infinite, and the Infinite is One
with me. No condition can hold me back, for I
am powerful and free. My Spiritual Powers rest in
the Ultimate, and the Ultimate rests in me.

49

The silent potency of the Light is re-creating my life
into radiant health, happiness and prosperity. The
living lushness of the Limitless Substance of the
Great Mother supplies me with all my needs.

50

I really am a beautiful person, because I am a child of the
Divine Mother, who is all beautiful, all symmetrical, all perfect.

51

The Inexhaustible Creativity of the Divine Mother
finds in me a fertile ground. I am rich in ideas,
thoughts and plans, and my life is a total success.

52

The rich Fertility and the calm Peace of the Living Light are at my disposal. I go about quietly and confidently to renew and re-create my life into radiant Bliss, Happiness and Fulfilment.

53

I order all my affairs according to the Creative Potential of the Infinite Light. All things are possible for me to accomplish, for the Living Light is the source of my Power.

54

I am never alone, for I am an inseparable part of the Greater Life of the Cosmos. I do not struggle by myself. In Him I live, move and have my Being.

55

My life is One with the Life of the Cosmos, and my consciousness is One with the Mind that moves all the stars throughout the Universe.

56

My life is patterned after the Great Cosmic Rhythm, and the Bounteous Infinite supplies all that I need. I am evolving with Boundless Space, and my life is God's own Self-Expression.

57

I am filled with the Knowledge of my infinite
Past, and I envisage my limitless Future. Mine
is the Power of Cosmic Comprehension.

58

I cooperate in the Divine Plan which God has for me. I am
One with the Cosmic Ebb and Flow, the cycles and rhythms
of the Cosmic Tides. My Evolution proceeds according
to Cosmic Law, and I understand the Cosmic Plan.

59

I recover the Wisdom of the Ages deeply buried in my
subconscious memories, and I walk the Path of Life
confidently, for I am blessed with God's beneficence.

60

The Eternal Consciousness in me is the Master of my Destiny.
I surrender my Life to the Action of the Divine Will.

61

I am protected and secure in the Hand of God, and
the Mysterious Forces of the Universe work out
my Destiny. I am One with the Eternal One.

62

Expansion, growth and opportunity come my way
daily. Full of confidence, I smile and am radiant, for
Life is but one great Gift for me. Happiness rises in my
breast like the phoenix bird out of sorrow's ashes.

63

My Will is resolute. My Life is unconquered. For who
can stop Omnipotence? Who can stand in Its way?

64

The ceaseless motion of Evolution drives me ever
onward to Perfection. The Law of Eternal Cycles unfolds
my unconquerable Will. I fear no evil. Limitations fade
away. My strength is Boundless. My Will is Absolute.

65

The handiworks of God spin through the
orbits of Space, and my birth and death is but
an interlude in my Heavenly Existence.

66

The pains and limitations of this life are but the stepping
stones to the Greater Life. The Real World is all around me.
I immerse myself in the Light of Cosmic Consciousness.

67

My Life is the rhythm of the movements of the
Cosmic Dancer, and my days are filled with
the Wonder of His Presence. "I am in Thee and
Thou art in Me"—O Unutterable Reality!

68

Mind is the Cause of every effect. The Mind of Light
masters all conditions and has dominion over all events.

69

All is Mind, and Mind is All. The Universe is a Mental Form.
The Universe is a Thought, thought out by the Mind of God.

70

Thought and Energy are One. Matter is condensed
Energy. Therefore, Matter and Mind are One.

71

Consciousness is the Root of all things, eternally coexistent
with Cosmic Space. Consciousness and Matter are
not two things, but behold one another in the Self.
Consciousness is the totality of Space and Time.

72

The Universe is alive. There is Life in everything, for all
that I see is but the Garments of Consciousness.

73

The Universe is the Dance of God, and all
that my eyes behold are but His Play.

74

Cosmic Intelligence governs the Universe. There is nothing
left to chance. The Supreme Intelligence that controls
the movements of the stars guides my Destiny also.

75

I am centred in the Life of God. The Being who
dwells at the Heart of the Universe and the Being
who dwells in my Heart are one and the same.

76

The Divine Mind heals me now. I set my feet firmly upon the
Path that leads to Discipleship and Cosmic Consciousness.

77

I am awakening to the Realization that it is the
Higher Self who is in charge of my personality.

78

I am no longer afraid to look at my faults and bad
habits. The Lightning Flash of the Sun of Illumination
gives me a clear view of Reality. I put behind myself
the past states of ignorance and wrongdoings
and walk consciously with the God of Truth.

79

I am in Thee, and Thou art in me, the One in All, the All
in One, the End in the Beginning, the Beginning in the
End, the past in the present, the present in the future,
and the future in the Eternal Now that never ends.

80

I resign my self-will into the sure Guidance of the Will of God.
In a flash of Clear Insight, I see into the Heart of the Universe.

81

I am awakening from this world of sorry illusions
and unrealities into the abiding World of Truth
and Eternal Glories. Abide Thou in Me.

82

My personal consciousness is being integrated
into the Universal Self. The Infinite Powers of
Superconsciousness await my call and I release them.

83

My tongue is a creative force. My will is a soaring energy.
My speech is a Spiritual Fire, releasing the God-Power
from within me. The Mouth of God speaks and His Words
are perfect, and I am One with His Perfect Eloquence.

84

The Spirit of Primal Fire awakens me now to the Knowledge
of my Eternal Self. The Voice of Fire transfigures me into the
real dimension of Superconscious Awareness. The Spirit of
God awakens me to a conscious experience of Immortality.

85

My Superconscious Self transfigures my mind and reveals
to my gaze the Ultimate Reality. I am awakened to the
Clarion Call of the Great Beyond, and resurrect from the
tombs of flesh and limited mind into the Limitless.

86

The Field of the Eternal awakens me from the
sleep of ignorance and urges me onwards to Self-
Realization. I am Consciously Immortal.

87

I am being reborn out of my old subconscious
and self-conscious minds into the New Image:
the Heavenly Man, the Perfect Self.

88

I invoke the Fire of Love to regenerate my personality
into the Perfect Image and Likeness of God. The
Heart of Fire awakens me to my own Divinity.

89

Beloved Father, this much I pray for: "Send forth Thy
Spirit and I shall be Re-Created, and Thou shalt renew
the face of the Earth." And Love shall prevail forever.

90

I bind myself to the One Will of the Universe. Of myself I do
nothing. My life depends on the Real World within me.

91

I attune my personality to the Universal Life around
me. My personal consciousness merges into the
Ocean of Life, and my mind is stilled in Ecstasy.

92

When the mind is still, the breath is still, and the Golden
Radiation becomes visible. When the activity of thought
ceases, and the emotions are laid to rest, and the senses
are poised, the Superconscious State is obtained.

93

The Suspended Mind has no objects to dwell upon—like
a sailing boat without a wind moves not along. When the
waves of thought are stilled, Liberation becomes possible.

94

Ecstasy is the Trance of the Soul when all activities of
body and mind are at rest. This Higher State is beyond the
understanding of the intellect. The Endless Miracles of the
Infinite Creation cannot be measured by the mind of Man.

95

Infinite Space is full of Gods waiting for my Coming to
take my place among Them. The Resplendent Shining
Ones dwell in Space on Shoreless Worlds, and I move
with Them, ever onward, into the Boundless.

96

I look forward to Limitless expansion, for my life is One
with the Life of the Limitless. Above and below stretches
the Boundless Life of God, and I am One with Him forever.

97

From my Mysterious Past I emerge into my Infinite
Future, shining like a star in the Eternal Heavens.

98

Let Love and Peace abide in every hour of my
days, and may I finally come to rest in Thee, O
Heart of Infinite Love! O Heart of Eternity!

99

Whatever I pay attention to, I become. My Consciousness shapes my Destiny. My thoughts are Magical. My life is Magical. I attain all my goals through Divine Magic.

100

Through Inner Seeing I perceive the Divine Worlds. I see things as they really are. By being ever-watchful, I set my life in order.

101

The Voice of Intuition teaches me the Divine Plan. I listen to His Instructions. By the Revelation of Truth I am set free from all ignorance and fear.

102

The Shining Holy Ones fix their gaze upon me. I turn my face towards the Sun of Illumination. I am being reborn into a new life, free from the limitations of time and place.

103

The darkness of ignorance and superstition vanishes away in the dawning Light of the Eternal Day. I am free from fear, free from disease, free even from the fear of death, for my life is One with the Eternal.

104

The Eternal Light-Bearer is always with me to
Light my Way. Every moment, I am under the
watchful supervision of the Great I AM.

105

The Sound Current of Liberation rings in my ears. The Voice
of Fire speaks to me the Eternal Truth. The whole Universe is
aflame with the Fire of Resurrection. Our God is a Consuming
Fire, and the Light of Truth burns away all illusions forever.

106

The Primal Will of the Cosmic Self guides me in
all my ways. The hand of the Eternal leads me
along the Path of Liberation. The Father of Light
guides me to perfect Union with my Beloved.

107

My feet are firmly set upon the Path and daily I follow the
Way of Return. A Bright Light shines upon the horizon
and my eyes open to Inner Vision. I see Beyond.

108

There never was a time when I was not. There
never shall be a time when I will not be. I and
my Father are One, for all Eternity.

109

My life is a periodic rhythm of the Cosmic Ebb and Flow. The One Life guides me ever onward to my perfect Destiny.

110

I am poised and calm through all actions. Resting under the Wings of Superconscious Guidance I achieve peace of mind, stillness in motion, peace amidst strife.

111

The Law of Compensation educates me in Intelligent Self-Direction. What I think, feel, and do, I become.

112

My mind is at peace. I surrender myself to the Cosmic Life. I have nothing to fear, for my life depends on God. I am secure in the sure Knowledge that my Beloved and I are One.

113

What I am today, I made myself from the past. Today, I make my tomorrow.

114

I Die daily, and I am Re-born daily. Every instant, I am undergoing change.

115

"That which was, is, and shall be" is the One Reality. Every detail of my life is but an expression of the Divine Presence.

116

Through the infallible Power of my Holy Guardian Angel, I achieve perfect Peace.

117

The trials, tests, and tribulations of my life are, in reality, lessons in my Faith. The One Reality guides me every moment of my life. My Higher Soul is with me.

118

The Power which tempts and destroys, is the same Power which renews and saves. The Magician of my Mind directs the Great Magical Agent to transform all negativity in my life into experiences of Joy and Happiness.

119

Appearances and falsehoods have no hold upon me. The Astral Light sets me free. The Magic Power of the Light pierces the veils of ignorance and fear.

120

A flash of Clear Vision reveals my True Identity. A beam of Clear Light from the Central Sun shatters the structure of my errors and ignorance.

121

I am awakening to the comprehension of Pure
Being. The delusion of separateness is destroyed by
my Intuition of the Oneness of the Beloved.

122

My Beloved reveals to me the Oneness of Being. I
am Liberated from the prison house of my body,
and roam freely in the Immeasurable Abyss.

123

"The Fire that burns not, but heals" removes my
delusions, and puts me face-to-face with my Beloved.

124

Nature reveals to me Her true Beauty. The
God-Power shines above my head. The Star of
Initiation removes all my fears and doubts.

125

My body-consciousness is transformed by my
mind. My bodily structure is changing to enable
me to experience Superconsciousness.

126

The door to the Invisible stands open before me. I
freely project myself into the Great Beyond.

127

The Sun of Life warms me. The Spiritual Sun regenerates me.
I am awakening into the Kingdom of Light that never fades.

128

The Inner Worlds open up Their Treasures to my purified gaze.
The Spirit of Primal Fire awakens me into the Higher Worlds.

129

All is Mind, the Mind is God, and God is
the Eternal Being of my Essence.

130

I rest my Life upon the Knowledge of the Eternal Being,
and Its perfect Law that guides the Universe forever.

———•———

Endnote

Creation—the Total Manifestation, the All-Reality—is divided into two major divisions or hemispheres, as is shown in the diagram *The Seven Great Planes of Being* (page vii). On the uppermost regions (the four formless Worlds of Light) are the Buddhic, Nirvāṇic, Paranirvāṇic, and Mahāparanirvāṇic Planes—amazing Light Universes, Light Solar Systems, Light Planets, and Light Beings completely beyond comprehension. That is one Reality, what we call the Transcendental Reality.

Then there is a huge gap or divide and another Creation (the three Lower Worlds) begins: the Mental Plane, the Astral Plane and the Physical Plane. Each plane has seven subplanes or dimensions, seven vibrational states of increasingly finer matter or energy within each plane. (We use the terms *planes, realms, worlds* and *dimensions* interchangeably.) Jesus referred to the multidimensionality of our Universe by the words: "In my Father's House there are many mansions" (John 14: 2).

The human being is therefore an immortal spiritual being called ĀTMAN (the Spirit) existing in the upper regions of Creation and at the same time a temporary manifestation called a *personality* living in the lower regions of Creation. And between the two there is a gap. The goal of the human evolutionary plan since the beginning of time until now is to bridge that gap, to go from *this* Creation to *that* Creation.

As a personality, we inhabit the three Lower Worlds. We live in a physical body made of the densest matter (solid, liquid, gas) of the lowest three subplanes of the Physical Plane. The higher four dimensions are called the etheric or etheric-physical dimensions, on which we exist in a subtle etheric-physical body.

Beyond the Physical Plane is the Astral Plane (or the Astral World), a world of feeling and desire, which consists of seven astral subplanes that correspond with the various heavens, hells and purgatories of the world religions. We exist on those subplanes in our astral body (which in Psychology is called the *subconscious mind*).

The lowest four subplanes of the Mental World are the realms of the lower, rational mind (our mental body), which shapes mental 'matter' into thoughtforms. The three higher subplanes (the Causal Worlds) are *formless* and correspond with the Higher Mind. As Human Souls, we dwell in our causal body in the three higher dimensions of the Mental Plane, whose seven subplanes are the true Heaven Worlds.

You, as the Soul, control your fourfold personality—the mental, astral, etheric and physical bodies. Your invisible bodies are just as real and solid on their own plane of manifestation as is your physical body on *this* plane. The Soul is the *Reincarnating Ego* because it takes on a new personality with each new incarnation.

SANSKRIT PRONUNCIATION GUIDE

~

VOWELS

A	AS IN FA**TH**ER
E	... THE**R**E
I	... **MACHINE**
O	... GO
U	... FU**LL**
Ṛ	... ME**RR**ILY (ROLLED)
Ṝ	... **MARINE**
AI	... **AI**SLE
AU	... H**AU**S (GERMAN)

LONG VOWELS

Ā, Ī, Ū

THE LONG VOWELS ARE PRONOUNCED THE
SAME AS THE SHORT VOWELS, BUT ARE
OF LONGER DURATION (TWO OR THREE
MEASURES). O AND E ARE ALWAYS SOUNDED
LONG. THE LONG Ö INDICATES A PROLONGED
SOUNDING.

SEMI-VOWELS

H	... **HEAR**
Y	... **Y**ET, LO**Y**AL
R	... **R**ED
V	... I**V**Y
	... MORE LIKE W WHEN
	FOLLOWING A CONSONANT
L	... **LULL**

GUTTURAL CONSONANTS

SOUNDED IN THE THROAT.

K	... **K**EEP
KH	... IN**KH**ORN
G	... **G**ET, DO**G**
GH	... LO**GH**UT
Ṅ	... SI**NG** (NASAL)

PALATAL CONSONANTS

SOUNDED AT THE ROOF OF THE MOUTH.

C	... **CH**UR**CH**
CH	... **CH**AIN
J	... **J**UMP
JH	... HE**DG**EHOG
Ñ	... SE**Ñ**ORITA

CEREBRAL CONSONANTS

SOUNDED WITH THE TONGUE TURNED UP TO
THE ROOF OF THE MOUTH.

Ṭ	... **T**RUE
ṬH	... AN**TH**ILL
Ḍ	... **D**RUM
ḌH	... RE**DH**AIRED
Ṇ	... **N**ONE

SANSKRIT PRONUNCIATION GUIDE
~

DENTAL CONSONANTS
SOUNDED WITH THE TIP OF THE TONGUE AT THE FRONT TEETH.

- T ... WATER
- TH ... NUTHOOK
- D ... DICE
- DH ... ADHERE
- N ... NOT

LABIAL CONSONANTS
SOUNDED AT THE LIPS.

- P ... PUT, SIP
- PH ... UPHILL
- B ... BEAR
- BH ... ABHOR
- M ... MAP, JAM

SIBILANTS
THE SIBILANTS ARE HISSING SOUNDS.

- S ... SAINT
- Ś ... SURE
- Ṣ ... SHOULD, BUSH

NASAL SOUNDS
THE NASAL SOUNDS ARE SOUNDED AS A HUMMING IN THE ROOT OF NOSE. THE FOLLOWING REPRESENT INCREASING DEGREES OF NASALIZATION:

M, Ṁ, Ṅ (NG), NG

ASPIRATED SOUNDS

- H ASPIRATED OUT-BREATHING
- Ḥ DEEPER OUT-BREATHING

VARIATIONS
THE VOWELS Ṛ AND Ṝ ARE SOMETIMES WRITTEN AS ṚI, RI OR RĪ WHEN FALLING AT THE END OF A WORD.
FOR EXAMPLE: SĀVITRĪ

SOME COMMON EXAMPLES OF ANGLICIZED SPELLINGS

CAKRA	... 'CHAKRA'
ṚṢI	... 'RISHI'
SVĀMĪ	... 'SWAMI'
ŚAKTI	... 'SHAKTI'
ĀKĀŚA	... 'AKASHA'
KṚṢṆA	... 'KRISHNA'
ĀŚRAMA	... 'ASHRAM'
AVATĀRA	... 'AVATAR'

ANGLICIZED SPELLINGS APPEAR IN THIS WORK ONLY IN THE CONTEXT OF POPULAR USAGE.

ABOUT THE AUTHOR

~

I mre Vallyon's extraordinary knowledge of human spirituality is derived not from scholarly research, but issues forth from his own Interior Realization. He spans the full spectrum of human experience: reaching through time, illuminating the great Spiritual Teachings and Sacred Languages of our planetary history while pointing the way to the future. Vallyon's work is one of synthesis. His writing is universal, not biased towards any particular religion or tradition.

Imre's vast Teaching has been recorded on over four thousand three hundred CDs and DVDs covering the total spectrum of Planetary Spirituality.

Imre Vallyon was awarded first place in the prestigious Ashton Wylie Charitable Trust Awards, as well as a gold medal in the 2009 Living Now Awards, for the four-volume spiritual treatise *Heavens and Hells of the Mind.*

SELECTED TITLES
~

The New Heaven and The New Earth
ISBN 978-0-909038-68-7

The New Planetary Reality
ISBN 978-0-909038-65-6

Planetary Transformation
ISBN 978-0-909038-61-8

Heavens & Hells of the Mind
ISBN 978-0-909038-30-4

The Magical Mind
ISBN 978-0-909038-11-8

The Warrior Code
ISBN 978-0-909038-64-9

The Sedona Talks
ISBN 978-0-909038-54-0

The Divine Plan
ISBN 978-0-909038-53-3

Heart to Heart Talks
ISBN 978-0-9038-55-7

The Art of Meditation
ISBN 978-0-9038-56-4

Please refer to our catalogue for a full list of products.

FOR MORE INFORMATION
~

Online
www.soundinglight.com
www.thefhl.org
info@soundinglight.com

Americas
PO Box 14094
San Francisco
CA 94114
United States of America

Asia-Pacific
PO Box 771
Hamilton 3240
New Zealand

Europe
PO Box 134
2000 AC Haarlem
The Netherlands

www.soundinglight.com

CPSIA information can be obtained at www.ICGtesting.com
Printed in the USA
LVOW06s0713110815

449418LV00002B/4/P

9 780909 038700